CORE BIBLICAL STUDIES

GOD IN THE NEW TESTAMENT

General Editors
Core Biblical Studies
Louis Stulman, *Old Testament*
Warren Carter, *New Testament*

Other Books in the Core Biblical Studies Series
The Apocrypha by David A. deSilva
The Dead Sea Scrolls by Peter Flint
Apocalyptic Literature in the New Testament by Greg Carey

Other Abingdon Press Books by Warren Carter
The New Testament: Methods and Meanings (with Amy-Jill Levine)
What Does Revelation Reveal? Unlocking the Mystery
The Roman Empire and the New Testament: An Essential Guide

*In solidarity
with all sufferers of domestic abuse—
women and men*

CORE BIBLICAL STUDIES

GOD IN THE NEW TESTAMENT

WARREN CARTER

Abingdon Press
Nashville

GOD IN THE NEW TESTAMENT
Copyright © 2016 by Abingdon Press

All rights reserved.

No part of this work may be reproduced or transmitted in any form or by any means, electronic or mechanical, including photocopying and recording, or by any information storage or retrieval system, except as may be expressly permitted by the 1976 Copyright Act or in writing from the publisher. Requests for permission can be addressed to Permissions, The United Methodist Publishing House, 2222 Rosa L. Parks Blvd., PO Box 280988, Nashville, TN 37228, or e-mailed to permissions@umpublishing.org.

Library of Congress Cataloging-in-Publication Data has been requested.

ISBN 978-1-4267-6633-6

All scripture quotations unless noted otherwise are taken from the New Revised Standard Version of the Bible, copyright 1989, Division of Christian Education of the National Council of the Churches of Christ in the United States of America. Used by permission. All rights reserved.

Scripture quotations marked NIV are taken from the Holy Bible, NEW INTERNATIONAL VERSION®. Copyright © 1973, 1978, 1984 by International Bible Society. All rights reserved throughout the world. Used by permission of International Bible Society.

Scripture quotations noted CEB are from the Common English Bible. Copyright © 2011 by the Common English Bible. All rights reserved. Used by permission. www.CommonEnglishBible.com.

16 17 18 19 20 21 22 23 24 25—10 9 8 7 6 5 4 3 2 1
MANUFACTURED IN THE UNITED STATES OF AMERICA

CONTENTS

General Preface vii

Chapter 1
Introduction: Constructing God-at-Work in the New Testament 1

Chapter 2
God-at-Work (Matt 1–2) 11

Chapter 3
God: Ultra Generous and Ultra Judgmental (Matt 22:1-14) 23

Chapter 4
The Good News and Empire of God (Mark 1:1-15) 33

Chapter 5
My God, My God, Why Have You Forsaken Me? (Mark 15:34) 45

Chapter 6
God and the Powerful and the Powerless (Luke 1:47-58; 6:20-26) 57

Chapter 7
Praying to What Sort of God? (Luke 11:1-13; Matt 6:5-15) 69

Chapter 8
How to Dishonor God (John 5:1-30) 81

Chapter 9
Cornelius, Peter, and an (Im)partial God (Acts 10:1–11:18) 93

Contents

Chapter 10
God Does Not Play Well with Other Gods (Acts 17:16-34) 105

Chapter 11
God Doesn't Throw Thunderbolts (Rom 1:16-32) 117

Chapter 12
God's Love Wins? (Rom 8:31-39; 11:25-32) 127

Chapter 13
*The Household of God and Its Male Guardians
(1 Tim 3:1-15; 2 Tim 2:14-26)*. 139

Chapter 14
God the Friend (Jas 4:1–5:6). 151

Chapter 15
All You Need Is Love? (1 John 3–4) 163

Chapter 16
God on the Throne (Rev 19:1-10; 21:1-8) 173

Chapter 17
Conclusion? 185

Notes. 197

General Preface

This book, part of the Core Biblical Studies series, is designed as a starting point for New Testament study.

The volumes that constitute this series function as gateways. They provide entry points into the topics, methods, and contexts that are central to New Testament studies. They open up these areas for inquiry and understanding.

In addition, they are guidebooks for the resulting journey. Each book seeks to introduce its readers to key concepts and information that assist readers in the process of making meaning of New Testament texts. The series takes very seriously the importance of these New Testament texts, recognizing that they have played and continue to play a vital role in the life of faith communities and indeed in the larger society. Accordingly, the series recognizes that important writings need to be understood and wrestled with, and that the task of meaning making is complicated. These volumes seek to be worthy guides for these efforts.

The volumes also map pathways. Previous readers in various contexts and circumstances have created numerous pathways for engaging the New Testament texts. Pathways are methods or sets of questions or perspectives that highlight dimensions of the texts. Some methods focus on the worlds behind the texts, the contexts from which they emerge and especially the circumstances of the faith communities to which they were addressed.

Other methods focus on the text itself and the world that the text constructs. And some methods are especially oriented to the locations and interests of readers, the circumstances and commitments that readers bring to the text in interacting with it. The books in this series cannot

General Preface

engage every dimension of the complex mean-making task, but they can lead readers along some of these pathways. And they can point to newer pathways that encourage further explorations relevant to this cultural moment. This difficult and complex task of interpretation is always an unfolding path as readers in different contexts and with diverse concerns and questions interact with the New Testament texts.

A series that can be a gateway, provide a guide, and map pathways provides important resources for readers of the New Testament. This is what these volumes seek to accomplish.

Warren Carter
General Editor

Chapter 1

Introduction: Constructing God-at-Work in the New Testament

I am on a road trip. God, or constructions thereof, seem to be everywhere—at least according to the billboards I see along the way. One billboard declares: "Let's meet at my house Sunday before the game. –God." The billboard presents a friendly, chatty God, a regular bloke who is one of us, who's hospitable, who likes football but with the gentle reminder that it's not the most important thing in life. I pass a more threatening and intimidating (or is it reassuring?) billboard that declares: "I'm closer than you think. –God." Another one presents God telling humans how to live: "Be faithful, loving, humble. –God." Apparently God uses billboards to communicate with humans. Another billboard urges me to "Explore God" as though God is a mystery or at least something to be poked and prodded. A bus goes by with "Warriors for God" displayed along the length of it. Apparently this God is in a battle, the general of an army for which humans can sign up. I pass a church sign that announces a friendly God who is with me all the time: "Exercise daily: Walk with God." Another billboard urges me to "Trust in the Lord," which reminds me of the tax bill I got recently from my local county treasurer declaring "In God we trust" on the envelope. I wasn't sure if that meant they were trusting God to enforce the payment of taxes (God does bad things to those who cheat on their taxes?) or that God would pay the taxes for me and I needn't bother to respond.

A Tale of Five Wits

I have found that people respond strangely when I tell them I am writing a book about God in the New Testament. Here's a sample:

Wit No. 1: "How many volumes do you plan? Seven or twelve?"

Wit No. 2: "Who's writing the book on whom? Wouldn't want to be you if you get it wrong."

Wit No. 3: "Ah, the ultimate mystery novel."

Wit No. 4: "'I believe in God, the Father almighty, creator of heaven and earth.' There you go, nothing more needs to be said."

Wit No. 5: "Which God?"

I know they were all trying to be funny in their own way. But at the same time, in these comments all of these folks were saying something about their understanding of God.

Wit No. 1 was drawing attention to the bigness of the topic and the incompleteness of any book on God, thereby highlighting the infinite and boundless nature of God.

Wit No. 2 was recognizing that the human–divine relationship is one of creature and creator and expressing concern that, in overreaching these boundaries, human hubris might provoke a wrathful and punishing response from an angry God.

Wit No. 3, perhaps knowing that I like to read mystery novels, was pointing to the mysterious and ultimately unfathomable ways of God. Apparently Wit No. 3 does not share the optimism of the English poet John Milton who set out in his epic poem *Paradise Lost* to "justify the ways of God to humans."

Introduction: Constructing God-at-Work in the New Testament

Wit No. 4 was quoting the Apostles' Creed, a confession formulated in the early centuries of the Christian church. Its first line confesses God as father (What sort? Close? Absent? Loving? Unaccountable? Punitive? Life-giving?), as all-powerful, as creator of the universe, and therefore as one who has a claim on everything and everyone. The creed echoes a traditional understanding of God as omnipotent (all-powerful), omniscient (all-knowing), and omnipresent (present everywhere). For Wit No. 4, that says it all about God.

Wit No. 5 reflects an insightful perspective that will recur throughout this book, namely that the New Testament presents God in different ways and that humans frequently create God in our image and according to our needs.

Beyond expressing their insights about God, these five wits were also raising another more basic question, namely, how to write a book about God. The topic is obviously huge, seemingly even infinite. And in Jewish, Christian, and Islamic traditions, humans have been thinking about and encountering God for millennia. The Hebrew Bible, or Old Testament, attests reflections that emerged in the various and changing circumstances of Israel's life in relation to God. Since then, across the Judeo-Christian traditions, classical philosophers, mystics, reformers, enlightenment philosophers, skeptics declaring the death of God, mental-health workers, psychiatrists, and contemporary theologians have continued to articulate understandings, experiences, and evaluations of God.[1] Such a wide span of human experience and reflection is way beyond this small book. We will restrict our attention to some New Testament presentations of God.

Yet even with this restricted focus, the question remains: how do we talk about God? As surprising as it may seem, not a lot of scholars have tried, at least in published form, to write books on presentations of God in the New Testament. One interpreter, Nils Dahl, famously called God a "neglected factor"[2] in studies of the New Testament. No one likes to be neglected.

Those who have tried to talk about God in the New Testament have taken several different approaches. One approach lists attributes of God. An obvious starting point for this approach comprises the four "God is..."

statements in the New Testament: "God is light" (1 John 1:5), "God is love" (1 John 4:8), "our God is a consuming fire" (Heb 12:29), and "God is Spirit" (John 4:24). We could add numerous other attributes: merciful, faithful, just, powerful, holy, wise, righteous, gracious, and so on. A variation on this approach identifies images and names associated with God (creator, father, king, judge, savior, etc.) and often appeals to the parables in the NT Gospels (a sower, a landowner, a slave owner, etc.).[3]

Another approach explores the diverse presentations of God in the various writings in the New Testament. This leads interpreters to examine how God is presented in the Gospels of Matthew, Mark, and John; across the two volumes of Luke and Acts; in the letters of Paul, particularly letters such as Romans and 1 Peter; and in writings such as Hebrews, James, and Revelation. Such studies helpfully underscore and elaborate the variety of presentations of God in the NT writings, as well as provide data for identifying common features.[4]

A third approach employs a different framework. This approach asks questions about the New Testament presentations from a perspective that anticipates the later church understanding of God as a trinitarian being. In the centuries after the NT writings, Christian theologians came to talk about God as one being who existed in three persons, God the Father or the Creator, God the Son or the redeemer, and God the Holy Spirit or sustainer. This third approach sees the beginnings of this trinitarian framework in the NT texts and identifies constructions of God, the interactions between God and Jesus, and interactions between the Spirit and God. This approach tends to harmonize the NT writings rather than highlight different presentations.[5]

All of these approaches are useful and have contributed insights into how God is presented in the New Testament. Since others have used them, I take a different approach in this book. My approach is marked by three distinctive features.

First, instead of focusing on the interaction between God, Jesus, and the Spirit, I want to focus on how the NT writers understood God and humans to interact or, more specifically, how they constructed God *to be active in the world and among humans*. Basic to this God-at-work approach is the recognition that the NT writers are not much interested in metaphysical questions about God's nature, as later theologians and philosophers have been (how is God God?). Rather NT writers are much more interested in understanding how humans experience God and in discerning what God might be doing among humans and in the world. To use other language, I am suggesting that NT constructions of God are functional rather than ontological. They are concerned with God's activity rather than God's being. They seek to articulate where, what, and how different writers understand God-at-work.

This focus on God-at-work is not only appropriate to the NT writings but also consonant with the interests and concerns that I often hear students articulate in the classroom. What in the world is God doing, if anything? Where *is* God-at-work? How do I know or recognize God's actions? Is God more absent than present? What does it mean to talk about God's activity or action in the contemporary world where we understand historical and scientific happenings in terms of cause and effect? If I believe in God, what sort of God do I believe in, on what basis, and what is this God doing? If God is active in the world, why is there so much evil and suffering? Contemporary students, like the NT writers, often wrestle with questions such as these with a sense of uncertainty or anxiety about the God to whom they have committed their lives in a cultural and intellectual context that seems regularly to distract from or undermine, rather than sustain, their commitment. I am not offering in this book an apologetic or defense of God. Rather, I name these questions as a way of focusing the discussion that follows. Engaging the NT presentations of God stimulates our own reflections and experiences.

A second distinctive feature of the approach in this book is its *textual* focus and organization. In the chapters that follow, I discuss texts of varying lengths from across the NT that highlight constructions of God-at-work. I have chosen texts from Matthew, Mark, Luke, John, Acts, Romans, 2 Timothy, 1 Peter, James, 1 John, and Revelation. Clearly I have not included every NT writing nor every reference to God. I am very aware that there are numerous other texts I could discuss, but limits on the size of this book mean I can't discuss all the texts. Sometimes I name some of these other texts in the questions at the end of each chapter. Needless to say, our topic is ultimately infinite and mysterious and no discussion about God in the NT can say everything that could be said. Each chapter offers a snapshot and each chapter could stand alone. Taken together, our sample of selected texts will allow us to notice at least some of the significant contours of the different constructions of God in the NT. I am not trying to build one composite image of God. The sequence of chapters or snapshots follows the canonical order of the selected texts.

In choosing to focus on particular texts, I recognize that these NT texts are *contextual* or *situational*. That means that when NT writers write about God, they do so in relation to particular circumstances, questions, or concerns that have arisen. Related to this awareness of the importance of situation is the recognition that NT writers do not write treatises about God or sustained systematic theological reflections. Rather, they write material that is relevant to the particular situations of their readers. One implication of the recognition of the situational nature of their discourse about God is that the NT writings do not say the same thing or even consistent things about God. They construct God in some different ways, and I want to be attentive to those differences as well as to the common affirmations that they may make. An advantage of discussing a number of texts is that it allows us to engage these contextualized constructions of God in some detail even when they are not especially appealing.

In addition to focusing on God-at-work in the world and among humans and on a sample of specific contextualized NT texts about God, a third feature of my approach consists of how I approach the interpretation of these New Testament texts. My interpretation is both *descriptive* AND *evaluative*. I take the New Testament texts very seriously, but I do not read them literally and with automatic compliance. I do not take a bumper sticker approach: "the Bible says it, I believe it, that settles it." If I read the New Testament that way, I would have to own slaves, think men are superior to women, be committed to genocide, and use violence to eliminate anyone who resisted when I imposed my ways on them. Various biblical writings, though, present God endorsing these practices and, as some argue, if it is good enough for God, then it's good enough for us! But of course, that is not morally acceptable. I don't think any of these practices is acceptable for human beings, let alone for God.

Some readers of the Hebrew Bible have drawn our attention to oppressive and tyrannical presentations of God in those writings. They have referred to passages such as the stories of Hagar (Gen 16; 21) and Tamar (2 Sam 13), for example, as "texts of terror" in which the constructions of God are terrible indeed.[6] But we have not often identified or thought about texts in the New Testament that might also be identified as "texts of terror." Yet as I will note throughout the discussions that follow, they exist.

I can recognize troubling constructions of God and even understand why NT writers might in particular contexts present God in these ways. But reading *evaluatively* means I cannot endorse their constructions or find them ethically acceptable. At heart in this approach are ethical questions about what sort of God might we believe in, about how we might understand the character and purposes of God-at-work, and about what way of life, what personal and communal identity, and what sort of person result from this belief. Both description AND evaluation provide a third crucial feature of this book's approach.

In the subsequent chapters, I often highlight these troubling, even terror-full, dimensions of constructions of God-at-work by referring to them as "**Red-flag alerts**" or by saying something like "the **Red flags** are waving." These references to "**Red-flag moments**" are a way of drawing attention to these very difficult and troubling constructions of God-at-work that need our further reflection.

Five Concluding Important Matters

One issue to note concerns the question of the relationship between talk about God and talk about Jesus. Or in theological terms, what is the relationship between theology and Christology? Christians have long recognized Jesus as the revealer and agent of God, so it would be easy, on this basis, to slip into writing a book about Jesus as though God has no life or existence apart from Jesus. But in the New Testament, Jesus never replaces or dislodges God. Jesus is, of course, prominent, and Jesus and God are linked, but they are also clearly distinguished. So in focusing on God, I will attempt to walk a line between paying too much attention to Jesus and paying too little attention to Jesus. Because New Testament writers frequently present Jesus as the agent, revealer, and locus of God's presence, purposes, and activity, understandings about God (theology) contextualize understandings about Jesus (Christology). Therefore, I recognize the need to hold these two things together. God is the origin, author, and sanction for Jesus. Or to put it bluntly, without God, Jesus is of no account. But the reverse is also true for the NT. In the New Testament, God is primarily linked to Jesus. God is the God of Jesus, the one who has raised Jesus from the dead and thereby inaugurated the new age that God will complete in fully establishing God's purposes. The particularity of God-at-work is declared by New Testament writers to be encountered in Jesus. Yet the two figures are distinct and not conflated.[6]

Second, in highlighting the variety of constructions of God in New Testament texts, I am not trying to construct one large image of God from the separate chapters. I am not trying to combine the different constructions of God into one image. For those who want a tidy confessional formula, this result will be messy, but it will be true to the New Testament texts.

A third important matter concerns gendered language for God. Much discussion of God, in the New Testament and since, has used male language for God. This language has included both male pronouns (his/he) and male images (king, father). Many women readers, for example, have found such references excluding or difficult to relate to in a positive way. Throughout, I will try not to use gendered language except when discussing NT texts that do so. But realistically, sometimes the occasional male pronoun will be necessary for the sake of understandable prose.

Fourth, I am not undertaking here an apologetic approach to God. There is a type of Christian discussion called *apologetics* that makes rational arguments for Christian faith, defends it against criticisms and objections,[7] and tries to convince people to become believers. The NT texts do not enter into discussions about whether God exists or not. They assume the existence and reality of God, and on this basis they focus on trying to discern where and how God is at work among humans. My emphasis is along the lines of describing and evaluating the constructions of God rather than making an argument for God's existence.

Finally, I should explain my interest in and perspective on this topic. I am a white male scholar raised in Aotearoa/New Zealand but living in the United States who teaches New Testament at a Christian protestant divinity school. As I have indicated above, I think the New Testament writings are very important, so in attending to what sorts of constructions of God they present, I read them as I indicated above, both descriptively and evaluatively. In taking this approach, I assume that this book is accessible to both those who believe in God and those who don't believe in God. I am writing for students in colleges and divinity schools, for study groups in churches, and for anyone else interested in how some New Testament writings talk about God.

With these factors in mind, we can turn to our first New Testament writing.

Further Reading

Andrew Das and Frank Matera, eds., *The Forgotten God: Perspectives in Biblical Theology* (Louisville: Westminster John Knox Press, 2002).

Frances Taylor Gench, *Encountering God in Tyrannical Texts: Reflections on Paul, Women, and the Authority of Scripture* (Louisville: Westminster John Knox, 2015).

Larry Hurtado, *God in New Testament Theology* (Nashville: Abingdon, 2010).

Jerome H. Neyrey, *Render to God: New Testament Understandings of the Divine* (Minneapolis: Fortress, 2004).

Neil Richardson, *Who on Earth is God? Making Sense of God in the Bible* (London: Bloomsbury, 2014).

Chapter 2

God-at-Work (Matt 1–2)

> *Read Matthew 1–2 before reading this chapter. Then refer to the text while you read the chapter.*

At first glance, God doesn't figure much explicitly in the opening two chapters of Matthew's Gospel. The chapters mention "God" explicitly just once (1:23), "the Lord" two times (1:22; 2:15), and "an angel of the Lord" four times (1:20, 24; 2:13, 19). Yet despite this lack of explicit references, I suggest God is the main character of these two chapters.

Another obstacle to this claim that God is the main character in Matthew 1–2 is the chapter's apparent focus on Jesus. We could divide the two chapters into four sections, all of which could be understood to center on Jesus:

- 1:1-17 The genealogy of Jesus

- 1:18-25 Jesus's conception and birth

- 2:1-12 Herod and the Magi respond to Jesus's birth

- 2:13-23 Joseph takes Jesus and Mary to Egypt and then to Galilee to protect Jesus against the murderous kings Herod and Archelaus

That makes some sense, I think, but it misses something more profound in these chapters, namely the central role of God. Here's another outline focusing on God.

- 1:1-17 God's purposes have been at work in Israel and the world

- 1:18-25 In this context, God graciously initiates the conception and commissioning of Jesus

- 2:1-12 God's activity is attested by the scriptures, ignored by the Jerusalem leaders, resisted by the Roman client king (Herod), and honored by the magi

- 2:13-23 God protects Jesus from the murderous violence of kings Herod and Archelaus

I will follow this second outline to look at how these two chapters construct God.

Matthew 1:1-17: God-at-Work in Israel and the World

Unless you are an ancestry buff, starting a story with seventeen verses and a list of forty-two generations is not very gripping. Yet these seventeen verses make a crucial, multifaceted contribution to the Gospel. They are not primarily about biology but theology. They show God-at-work in mixed and at times contradictory ways as life-giving, purposeful, selectively interventionist, active yet absent, inclusive yet exclusive, omnipresent though invisible, and busy in accomplishing God's purposes.

The passage's most basic, and perhaps controversial, claim is that human history is not random. The text claims that despite all appearances to the contrary, in daily lives and in world events, God is at work. Often, the genealogy shows, God works with unlikely characters and in unlikely circumstances. As one example, verses 11-12 mention the deportation of Israel's elite to Babylon in the year 587 BCE. This event followed the Babylonian destruction of Jerusalem and its temple. It was a 9/11–type event on steroids that seemed to bring an end to the nation. It was understood that when armies went to war, so did their gods. In the face of Babylonian

God-at-Work (Matt 1–2)

military power, it seemed that God was weak, helpless, defeated, and disinterested. God seemed unable to deliver on God's promises to protect the people against a foreign army. Yet mysteriously and powerfully, some fifty years later in 539 BCE, the biblical authors see God-at-work when the Persian ruler Cyrus, a Gentile, returns the people to their land, allowing for the rebirth of the nation (Isa 44:28–45:1). Who would have thought God could do that?

Interestingly, the genealogy relies on 20/20 hindsight to discern God-at-work. Even in situations when God seems to be absent or powerless, the genealogy discerns God-at-work.

Verse 1 introduces Jesus by associating him with two big figures in Israel's history, Abraham and David. Both of them were big because God had chosen and commissioned them as agents of God's purposes. God appoints Abraham to "'go from your country . . . to the land that I will show you. I will make of you a great nation . . . and in you all the families of the earth shall be blessed'" (Gen 12:1, 3). God promises to work through Abraham for two ends: to create a great nation and to bless all the families of the earth. The first end is exclusive (one nation, Israel, not, for example, the Roman Empire), the second is all-embracing ("all the families"; Gentiles). The two purposes seem to stand in tension.

The rest of the genealogy shows God's continued quixotic and unpredictable work. God rejects the cultural pattern of the privileged first-born male by electing Isaac rather than his older brother Ishmael, Jacob instead of first-born Esau, and Judah, the fourth-born of eleven brothers who originated the twelve tribes of Israel (Matt 1:3-4). God seems to skip the generations between Joram and Uzziah (1:8). And there is no mention of famous figures like Moses or any of the prophets.

Yet God's indiscriminate and inclusive blessing of all people embraces both Israel and Gentile nations like Babylon (Matt 11:11b-12), men (most of the names) and women (five women in Matt 1:3, 5, 16, unusual in a genealogy but not unique), giants in the tradition like Abraham and David (Matt 1:2, 6) and nobodies forgotten by the tradition (Matt 1:13-15), rulers and ruled (Matt 1:6-11), the morally upright, the morally ambiguous (David), and the evil (Manasseh). Throughout, God's intention is, apparently, to bless all people with plentiful fertility, food, health, prosperity, and freedom from imperial rules (outlined in Deut 28–29).

This intention, of course, did not always happen as the prominence of kings in the line of David indicates. God chose David as "a man after [God's] own heart" (1 Sam 13:13-14) to represent God's rule among the people (2 Sam 7). Royal psalms like Psalm 72 celebrate the king's job description in representing God's rule in actions such as defending the poor, delivering the needy, and resisting oppressors (Ps 72:4). On their good days, kings enacted God's good, just, and life-giving purposes.

But of course, powerful kings, including David, got distracted and did not often have good days. Instead of using their power for the good of others, they used it for their own benefit. Matthew 1:6b-11 identifies fifteen kings between David and Jeconiah. Only two of them, kings Hezekiah and Josiah, are evaluated in the books of Kings and Chronicles as "good kings" faithful to God's purposes. David was a mixed bag and Manasseh is judged to be one of the most sinful (Matt 1:10). Yet the relentless list of naughty kings, the narrative of failed kingship, and the action of the imperial power Babylon in destroying Jerusalem and removing the kings in 587 BCE provides a context in which God's determination and power will be displayed.

In the face of such evil and contradictory actions, God's commitments mean that God can work with and around human rebellion and faithlessness. God is not involved only with holy people. In fact, God seems not to differentiate between the righteous and the unrighteous, saints and sinners, but embraces all in God's purposes.

Through the genealogy, then, God, though never mentioned, is shown to be present, very busy, and interventionist though invisible. But the genealogy constructs God operating with a clear agenda. God is doing all of this work, so verses 1-17 declare, with an eye on the coming of Jesus, who is mentioned at the beginning in verse 1 and at the end in verses 16-17. The genealogy spins Israel's history for this end. While God is shown to want to bless all the families (Abraham), in the end, the genealogy tries to coopt God by linking God exclusively to Jesus to continue God's work of blessing and ruling.

The genealogy thereby creates a contradiction, constructing God initially as very inclusive yet finally as very exclusive and excluding. It fails in the end to live up to its initial construction of God as indiscriminate in bestowing blessing on all (Abraham) by apparently narrowing the focus to Jesus as God's agent.

The Gospel, though, does not forget this initial presentation of God. Five chapters later in the Sermon on the Mount, Jesus makes this comment about God's indiscriminate loving and blessing for all:

> "You have heard that it was said, 'You shall love your neighbor and hate your enemy.' But I say to you, Love your enemies and pray for those who persecute you, so that you may be children of your Father in heaven; for he makes his sun to rise on the evil and on the good and sends rain on the righteous and on the unrighteous." (Matt 5:43-45)

Matthew 1:18-25: God Graciously Initiates the Conception and Commissioning of Jesus

The genealogy has introduced Jesus as the goal of God's purposes. Now it shows the origin of Jesus in the gracious action of God, not in the sexual activity of Joseph and Mary. In fact, five times in these seven verses the passage affirms God's gracious initiative in the origin of Jesus.

First, the narrator says Mary becomes pregnant "before they lived together," which is polite Bible-talk for "before they had sex":

> When his mother Mary had been engaged to Joseph, but before they lived together, she was found to be with child. (Matt 1:18b)

Inquiring minds of course want to know, "How did THAT happen?" So immediately verse 18 adds an explanation, "from the Holy Spirit" (1:18c), the second claim of God's involvement. Just exactly how the Spirit accomplished this conception is not explained, but the verse makes one thing very clear. Through the Spirit, God initiates the conception of Jesus. It was not uncommon in the ancient world for people to claim that gods were involved in the conception of outstanding humans like Alexander the Great, the Roman founder Romulus, and the Roman emperor Augustus. God's action places Jesus in the company of the greats.

The third statement of God's initiative comes when an angel of the Lord repeats the claim: "an angel of the Lord appeared to him in a dream and said, 'Joseph, son of David, do not be afraid to take Mary as your wife, for the child conceived in her is from the Holy Spirit'" (Matt 1:20).

The fourth claim comes with an appeal to scripture as revealing God's purpose: "All this took place to fulfill what had been spoken by the Lord through the prophet" (Matt 1:22).

And the scene ends with a fifth statement that claims Joseph and Mary did not have sex: "but [Joseph] had no marital relations with her until she had borne a son" (Matt 1:25).

If something is repeated five times in seven verses, it must be important. It must be important. It must be important. It must be . . . Repeated five times. The point here is not that God is opposed to sex. The Song of Songs indicates otherwise. The point is that Jesus enters the world of humans at God's initiative. The scene sets God's stamp of approval on Jesus. God sanctions Jesus. Jesus is God's agent.

But—**Red-flag alert**—we have to pause and recognize something troubling. The scene says nothing about Mary's willingness to become pregnant. There's nothing here about Mary's consent. To become pregnant when you are betrothed (like engagement) and you're not pregnant by your husband-to-be causes obvious personal and social problems (Matt 1:19). It's a source of shame from which it's very hard to recover. Imagine the social shame, the gossip, and the disbelief if you start claiming divine intervention. To describe God's intervention in or invasion of Mary's life as only gracious seems one-sided.

The narrative does not pause to raise or address these questions. Rather it moves on to Jesus's life-work. What is he to do? Matthew 1:21-23 spells out Jesus's job description as God's representative:

> "You are to name him Jesus, for he will save his people from their sins" . . .
> And "they shall name him Emmanuel" which means "God is with us."

The baby is given two names, "Jesus" and "Emmanuel." The names are not chosen out of a baby book or from a TV show because they are popular, weird, or cute. The names are very pragmatic; they are slogans. They convey Jesus's job description, his life's work, his mission. The name "Jesus" is the Greek form of the Hebrew name "Joshua," and it means "God saves." This link is important because it immediately says something about the scope and type of "saving" Jesus is to do. To save from sins does not just mean forgiving me for the things I say and do that are hurtful or rescuing me from stupid things I might do. Evoking Joshua paints a much broader, international picture of God-at-work saving people from all sorts of sins in communities and nations. The genealogy in Matthew 1:1-17 has shown God-at-work across generations involving numerous situations and people, which includes saving the people from the imperialist aggression of Babylon. Jesus continues God's work.

And when Jesus is doing this work as God's agent, he is making God present among humans. So he is named "Emmanuel," which means God is with us. Very important here is that Matthew 1:23 quotes from Isaiah 7, in which Isaiah shows the vast extent of God-at-work, and thereby helps to define Jesus's mission.

In Isaiah 7, the nation of Judah is under threat from the northern powers of Israel and Syria. What should Judah and its king Ahaz do? Fight? Make alliances? Or, according to Isaiah, trust God to ensure the nation's future? In support of the latter option, the prophet declares that a young woman in the royal family will give birth to a baby boy who will be Judah's future ruler. (In its context of Isaiah 7, this is not originally a reference to Jesus). The child, to be named Emmanuel, is God's promise to be present with the people, that the nation has a future and will survive this crisis, and that God will protect it and ensure the next generation. Evoking this scene shows the communal and international extent of Jesus's saving activity as the agent of God-at-work with people living among the Roman Empire.

Matthew 2:1-12: Responses to God-at-Work

Jesus's birth occurs in Matthew 2:1. The text does not dwell on it; there are no details about baby showers, the length of Mary's labor, how well Joseph coped or not, the baby's weight or length, what percentage of costs the insurance covered. Rather, the chapter's focus centers on how people respond to God-at-work through his agent Jesus, who is designated a king and is to manifest God's saving presence and rule (1:21-23).

First, some "wise men from the East" follow a star to Jerusalem, the center of the rule of King Herod, the Rome-sanctioned king of the Jews. They ask an unwise question about the whereabouts of "the child who has been born king of the Jews?" (Matt 2:2). In Herod's hometown, this is not a smart move. These "wise men" are "magi," a priestly class who served rulers. They were ambivalent figures. They were astrologers skilled and learned in gaining knowledge and power from interpreting the heavens. With this knowledge, they could support or destabilize rulers. Yet they had mixed PR. Some people took them very seriously; others mocked them for speaking nonsense.

Here, despite their unwise question, they are observant enough to notice a special star, knowledgeable enough to interpret this natural phenomenon as signifying the birth of a new king, motivated enough to travel far, courageous enough to enter Herod's territory, discerning enough to know that homage is appropriate (Matt 2:3, 10-11), and in tune enough with God's voice to resist Herod's command to be his spies (2:8-9, 12). As Gentiles aligned with another religious tradition and set of practices, they discern God-at-work and honor God's initiative.

Second, King Herod responds very differently. He is a puppet ruler or representative of the Romans in this province of the Roman Empire. He has sustained his more-than-thirty-year rule by astutely (re)aligning himself with changing power formations in Rome. He has a reputation for ruthlessness and paranoia, so he is frightened by hearing about the birth of another king (Matt 2:3). He resorts to a toolkit typical of ruthless, paranoid rulers. He has allies to gain knowledge about this king (2:4) and spies to locate him (2:8), and he lies about wanting to honor Jesus (2:8). His response is self-protective, hostile, resistant—and it will get worse in the second half of the chapter.

Third, Herod's allies are the Jerusalem leaders, the "chief priests and scribes of the people" (Matt 2:3). We immediately think of these people as clergy-type figures. But in the first century, they were also the political and social leaders of Judea and held much power, wealth, and status. The chief priests ran the temple and ordered the nation's life. The scribes were the legal experts, interpreters, and teachers. They were partners with Herod in ruling the nation. They represented its traditions and culture. So they interpreted the tradition for Herod, pointing to Micah 5:2 as indication that a ruler will come from David's town of Bethlehem.

But what do they then do? Nothing! They do not make any connection with Jesus. They do not go to Bethlehem to honor him. They ignore him and disappear. They do not know to read the scriptures in relation to Jesus.

At heart, they cannot discern God-at-work. Herod is threatened by God-at-work. The wise men or magi welcome God-at-work.

Matthew 2:13-23: God Protects Jesus But ...

Herod's resistance and paranoia expressed through his allies, spies, and lies drives this section—until Herod dies. His death is mentioned three times in 2:15, 19, and 20. It is not directly attributed to God, but that is a fair inference. God thwarts him and protects Jesus. **Red-flag alert**—does God really eradicate ruthless political leaders?

In this situation of the danger posed by Herod, God intervenes through an angel and a dream. By these means, God reveals to Joseph Herod's desire to destroy Jesus and sends him and "the child and his mother" to safety in Egypt (Matt 2:13). Word for word, Joseph obeys (Matt 2:14). This of course is not the first time in the biblical tradition that God has been involved in political matters and protected God's agent from a tyrannical ruler. The reference to Egypt recalls God's protection of the child Moses from Pharaoh (Exod 1–3). The biblical citation of Hosea 11:1 recalls the exodus of the people from Egypt and freedom from the tyrant Pharaoh. Jesus is associated with these great expressions of God-at-work in powerfully resisting tyranny and liberating the people.

But then a huge theological problem emerges in the narrative's presentation of God. Herod, recognizing his failure to turn the wise men into spies, resorts to another strategy employed by oppressive tyrants: murderous violence against his own people. Having learned about Bethlehem from the leaders of Jerusalem, he seeks to wipe out any threat from Jesus by sending troops to Bethlehem to kill all the baby boys two years old and under in its region (Matt 2:16-18).

The narrative hints at the fear and terror, the profound grief and mourning, the hopelessness and despair that resulted among the local population when Herod's terrorist troops moved into the region: "wailing and loud lamentation, Rachel weeping for her children; she refused to be consoled, because they are no more" (Matt 2:18).

Here's the **Red-flag alert**. God keeps his chosen agent Jesus safe from this terror around Bethlehem because God has directed Joseph to take him to Egypt. But the cost of providing this protection for Jesus was the innocent lives of the babies slaughtered around Bethlehem. The prayers of the parents for safety for their babies went unanswered. God did not intervene. God was not present in power to deliver them. God-at-work could thwart Herod's threat to Jesus but not the danger to the babies of Bethlehem. The weeping and mourning of the local population expresses and protests the injustice, the inactivity, the indifference, the powerlessness, the absence of God.

What can we say? Perhaps silence in the face of such tragedy is the best response. Another starting point is to note the tragedy and terrible human suffering, repeated on our planet daily without ceasing. Many folks at the mercy of cruel forces and uncontrollable events have questioned where God's power and love might be in the midst of such circumstances. Many have experienced its absence.

A further starting point might be to note that God's purposes for a just world are not yet complete. We have seen God's intentions expressed in Abraham to bless the entire world, but that reality is not yet in place. Of course, we have to ask, "Why not?" Is God not powerful or vigilant enough? Or in the lament of the psalmist, "How long, O LORD?" (Pss 13:1; 35:17; 79:5; 89:46).

A third starting point is to recognize our own culpability. Why do we humans continue to treat one another in such ways? But that doesn't explain every situation. Being human in an imperfect and broken world—a world not yet repaired by God—leaves us vulnerable and at risk in all sorts of unexplained and often unanticipated ways. We might understand God to mourn and grieve with us, to be present with us in such situations. But nevertheless, "s*** happens" and none of us escapes.

Matthew 1:19-20 twice refers to Herod's death, indicating that God eventually thwarts Herod. Of course, it's too late for the families around Bethlehem, and his death does not restore life to the dead babies. But at least his tyranny does not last forever. Again God intervenes and, through an angel and a dream, directs the protector Joseph to take "the child and his mother" back to Egypt. Again, word-for-word, Joseph faithfully obeys (Matt 2:20-21).

But all is not well. God might have thwarted Herod, but Herod's death is not the death of evil and tyranny. The narrative employs scary words: "Archelaus was ruling over Judea in place of his father Herod" (Matt 2:22). Like father, like son. Joseph discerns the danger, and again guided by God, he withdraws north from Judea to the town of Nazareth in Galilee.

He does not, though, find serenity and safety. Galilee has its own dangers. When he grows up, Jesus will identify with John the Baptist, whose fiery, prophetic message aggravates other social leaders like Pharisees and Sadducees (Matt 3:7) and Israel's Rome-appointed and sanctioned ruler, Herod Antipas (4:12; 14:1-12). John criticizes Herod Antipas, is arrested, and is then executed. John, like the babies of Bethlehem, is another victim of a tyrant's power. And like them, he is not saved by an apparently indifferent and powerless God (14:1-12).

And perhaps—another **Red-flag moment**—we should spare a thought for Joseph: ordered to marry a woman he did not get pregnant, raise a child who is not his, and relocate twice—all in the name of obeying God. Is God a cruel master for the subordinate Joseph or is Joseph blessed to be a servant of God?

Questions for Reflection/Discussion

1. Summarize the diverse ways God is constructed in Matthew 1–2. How do you make sense of the contradictions?

2. Suffering and tragedy haunt the human experience, raising questions about God's powerful presence and powerless absence, human responsibility, and the mystery of human vulnerability ("S*** happens"). What do you make of this?

3. Psalm 24 declares, "The earth is the Lord's and the fullness thereof." How do chapters 1–2 exemplify or contradict this claim of God's sovereignty? Do you agree with the psalmist?

Further Reading

Warren Carter, *Matthew and the Margins: A Sociopolitical and Religious Reading* (Maryknoll, NY: Orbis Books, 2000), 51–89.

Richard Horsley, *The Liberation of Christmas: The Infancy Narratives in Social Context* (New York: Crossroad, 1989).

Chapter 3

God: Ultra Generous and Ultra Judgmental (Matt 22:1-14)

> *Read Matthew 22:1-14 before reading this chapter. Then refer to it while you read the chapter.*

Two quite different presentations of God coexist in this parable of the king who throws a wedding party for his son. God is very generous and very harsh, very gracious and very judgmental. There's a **Red flag** waving.

The parable occurs in the last section of Matthew's Gospel. Jesus entered Jerusalem on Palm Sunday (21:1-11) and immediately enters into conflict with the Jerusalem leaders (21:23, 45-46). They have been at odds throughout the Gospel. Now the conflict is ramped up, and it will result in Jesus's death in chapter 27. Fueling this conflict is a series of three parables that Jesus tells in 21:28–22:14.

- Parable of the two sons: 21:28-32

- Parable of the wicked tenants who won't pay the rent: 21:33-44

- Parable of the king who throws a wedding feast for his son: 22:1-14

Jesus tells these parables against the Jerusalem-based leaders (not against all Israel; Matt 21:45). The parables announce God's judgment on the

Jerusalem-based leaders because they have not been receptive to his activity. The parable of the king and his wedding feast for his son is the third of the three.

A parable creates a comparison. The word "parable" comes from two Greek words. It literally means to "throw (one thing) alongside (another)." So in this parable, the kingdom of heaven is set alongside or compared to the situation of the parable. Matthew has presented the kingdom of heaven or the rule or empire of God as central to Jesus's activity (4:17). It enacts his commission to manifest God's saving presence (Matt 1:21-23). It is a way of talking about God-at-work through Jesus, about how God's presence or purposes or rule are active through him among human beings. This parable creates a comparison with the actions of the king so as to highlight something important about God's rule.

Generosity, along with a lack of reality, marks the first six verses. The king plans a wedding feast for his son and sends out his slaves to inform his elite courtiers and clients to "save the date." If we have been reading through the Gospel, we readily recognize the technique of allegory where one thing stands for another. The previous Gospel narrative has identified the king as God. The son is Jesus. The wedding banquet is variously God's covenant with God's people or a final banquet that celebrates God's reign in which all people participate in a feast marked by God's abundant goodness and fertility (read Isa 25:5-10a). The invited guests are Israel's leaders. The slaves are the prophets sent to call rulers and leaders back to their roles of enacting God's purposes for the people and away from their self-interested structures and practices.

We might pause—the **Red flag** is waving—and notice how the parable reinscribes fundamental societal structures, practices, and values from its first-century world without any reflection on them or critique of them. It is monarchical in centering on a king and patriarchal in ignoring the queen. It upholds a hierarchical structure with king at the top, then his clients and courtiers, and finally slaves at the bottom of society. Its use of slaves employs a structure in which slaves were always subject to their master's will in controlling them body and soul. And their bodies are subject here to murderous violence at the hands of some courtiers and clients

(Matt 22:6). The unquestioning use of this hierarchical structure, including the inhumane institution of slavery, might suggest God's approval—unfortunately.

In an insulting act, the invited leaders reject the king's invitation (Matt 22:3b). It is more than rude; it is a dishonoring and rebellious act to refuse the king's invitation to the party of the year. Kings can expect from courtiers and clients public displays of loyalty and deference; in turn, courtiers and clients can expect favors and benefits from the king. Their insulting refusal, however, has blown this reciprocity to bits. The next move ought to be from the insulted and dishonored king, an act of retaliation and retribution that puts them back in their place of duty and indebtedness and reminds them of who is the boss.

Instead, surprisingly, the king absorbs their insults, and with generosity, issues a second invitation (Matt 22:4). The king/God ignores the conventions of retaliation, acts with freedom, and takes a different path. Yet by the social conventions of honor and power, his response makes him look weak, desperate, even needy. Perhaps this response provides incentive for them to again refuse the king's invitation. Things escalate. Some simply ignore him and disrespectfully attend to their own business activities that sustain their power, wealth, and status, while others resort to violence and attack and kill the king's slaves (22:6). It's an extreme way to say no to a wedding invitation.

But now the king's generosity runs out. It is replaced by violent and destructive revenge. The enraged king sends troops to kill those clients who have insulted him and to burn their city (Matt 22:7). His response is devastatingly violent. Unfurl the **Red flag.**

The allegory of the parable, along with knowledge of imperial ways, of biblical perspectives, and of historical events, points here to a reference to the Roman destruction of Jerusalem in the year 70 CE. Destroying cities was a common means of subjugating and punishing defiant people. The biblical tradition interpreted the Babylonian destruction of Jerusalem in 587 BCE (recall Matt 1:11-12) as God's punishment on the city and its leaders for being unfaithful to God. So the prophet Jeremiah declared:

> Therefore thus says the LORD of hosts: Because you have not obeyed my words, I am going to send for all the tribes of the north, says the Lord, even for King Nebuchadnezzar of Babylon, my servant, and I will bring them against this land and its inhabitants . . . I will utterly destroy them, and make them an object of horror . . . This whole land shall become a ruin and a waste, and these nations shall serve the king of Babylon seventy years. (Jer 25:8-11)

There is a similar interpretation in 1 Kings 9:6-9:

> "If you turn aside from following me, you or your children, and do not keep my commandments and my statutes that I have set you before you, but go and serve other gods, and worship them, then I will cut Israel off from the land that I have given them and the house that I have consecrated for my name I will cast out of my sight and Israel will become a proverb and a taunt among all peoples. This house will become a heap of ruins; everyone passing by it will be astonished, and they will say, "Why has the Lord done such a thing to this land and to this house?' Then they will say: "Because they have forsaken the LORD their God, who brought their ancestors out of the land of Egypt, and embraced other gods, worshiping and serving them; therefore the LORD has brought this disaster upon them."

In the light of this sort of thinking about God-at-work, the parable interprets the Roman destruction of Jerusalem and burning of the temple in 70 CE as God's punishment on the leaders of Jerusalem for their rejection of God's son, Jesus.

Our questions may be not so much "Why has the Lord done such a thing?" but "*what sort of God* does such things?" Or "what sort of tradition constructs God-at-work in this way?"

The parable presents God as a copycat, imitating imperial tyrants who destroy those who dishonor them. It constructs God as violent, vindictive, revengeful, and lacking mercy in eradicating the leaders of Jerusalem who had not received Jesus. God appears as a terrorist. God is constructed as a "do it my way or I'll pummel you into oblivion" sort of character. But worse, it also presents God as oblivious to the fallout of God's actions. It's bad enough that God appears as a bully in destroying his opponents, but of course, it is not just the leaders who are impacted when a city is destroyed. God seems indifferent to the lives of numerous innocent citizens who are collateral damage. The **Red flag** is waving. This is a text of terror.

God: Ultra Generous and Ultra Judgmental (Matt 22:1-14)

Beyond outrage at the presentation of God as a vengeful king who destroys the leaders of Jerusalem and innocent citizens, can we make sense of this presentation of God? Of course, we could appeal to the fact that other Jewish writers also interpreted Jerusalem's destruction as God's punishment. The Jewish historian Josephus does so. So too do other writings appearing at the same time as Matthew late in the first century such as 4 Ezra and 2 Baruch. These writings, though, are not Christian writings. They do not see God's punishment as having anything to do with rejecting Jesus.[1] But they do see God-at-work in punishing Jerusalem.

Others would say that what we are seeing in Matthew's parable scene is God acting justly. Having sent out not just one invitation but two invitations, God must judge and punish those who have ignored or insulted those invitations. In other words, some argue, it's the leaders' own fault. They have brought this on themselves. They forced God to punish them.

But there is something troubling with this logic, is there not? How far can we generalize this principle that "historical disasters express God's punishment"? Does every plane crash, every hurricane or tsunami, every crop failure, every cancer-ridden body, every tyrant who practices genocide, every totalitarian regime that murders its opponents, every multinational corporation that exploits its workers, every terrorist attack, every car accident express God's punishment? Or to put it in very personal terms, did my baby die because God was punishing me?

Such a nexus of "disaster equals divine punishment" seems too simplistic. What role do natural processes play? What role do human decisions and freely-chosen actions play? If the Babylonians or Romans decide to attack Jerusalem and overrun it with superior military power to achieve dominance, isn't an explanation in military terms sufficient? Does it have anything to do with God causing it? Are we humans puppets manipulated by God?

Of course, this way of thinking may have some value. If we recognize that God works in mysterious ways, we can never rule it out. And we humans always have the option of making meaning of our lives and the circumstances of our world in relation to God. So the nexus of "disaster equals divine punishment" might be a way of making sense of a tragedy. It can be a way of getting our attention. It can provoke some soul-searching in our lives. God may not cause it, but we may discern some significance in an event in relation to God. Some might even find in such experiences signs of God's care and love. Anger can be an expression of care, that someone—God—wants something better for us and from us.

But again, caution is necessary. We can't assume that a positive outcome from tragedies is automatic or inevitable. That would be to trivialize the human dimensions of tragedies. They result in destruction, brokenness, bitterness, and woundedness that may or may not ever heal.

Recognizing all of this, here's the central issue that bothers me. The parable identifies both God's grace and God's judgment. But what's the relationship between God's punitive judgment and God's love? Does God's violently-expressed judgment overwhelm, even negate, God's promise of blessing all the families of the earth (see discussion of Matt 1:1)? Or does the indiscriminate and ever generous love and mercy of God bestowed extravagantly on the "evil and on the good . . . on the righteous and on the unrighteous" win the day (Matt 5:45)? Love does not eliminate punishment, but punishment without love is a scary prospect. A vulnerable human in the hands of an angry God (to reword Jonathan Edward's concern) is frightening if judgment, not love, has the final say.

New and Unlikely Invitations

Reading on in the parable provides further exploration of this interaction between love and judgment. The king's anger immediately dissipates in reaching out to a much more inclusive audience (Matt 22:8-10). The king does not change his mind about the powerful leaders—they remain "unworthy" and they are not offered any further chance. Rather, the king turns his attention elsewhere. The king goes looking for others with whom to celebrate the son's marriage. He sends his slaves to the survivors in the city, those living on the streets, the homeless, the poor, "both good and bad." Surprisingly, even scandalously, they are invited as the king's new guests who fill the wedding hall (22:10). Kings don't usually associate with, let alone host, the riff-raff. Again, he acts in a surprisingly dishonorable way in this act of freedom, a contrary-to-normal way of behaving. He performs an inclusively merciful act. This is God-at-work.

If the parable ended here, we could celebrate a happy ending. God's mercy and love triumph over God's judgment. But verses 11-14 give us some pause, some discomfort again with the **Red flag** still waving.

The wedding party is underway, and the king notices among the guests one "who was not wearing a wedding robe" (Matt 22:11-12). Again, the parable enters the realm of the unrealistic. How on earth can the king expect his guests from off the streets in the midst of the smoldering ruins of the burned city to have access to wedding garments? Did all these other "guests" somehow come up with a wedding garment but not this poor guy?

We could explain away this lack of realism by saying the allegory takes over. The wedding garments highlight that those who share in the king's/God's mercy must be "worthy." Clothing often represents a way of life—like baptismal garments or putting on Christ in a new way of life marked by good works, acts of love, and faithful living. On this reading, the guest singled out by the king does not exhibit this way of life. In addition to lacking a life of faithful actions, "he was speechless." He cannot offer appropriate words of appreciation or acknowledgement for the king's/God's goodness and mercy.

The king's anger and violence return. There seems to be no understanding of or patience for the man's situation. There's no second chance. The king does not send him off to try and find an acceptable garment somewhere. Or even more realistically, the king does not provide him with a garment. What sort of God turns away those whom God has invited and admitted to the feast?

The king/God orders the man thrown out "into the outer darkness, where there will be weeping and gnashing of teeth" (Matt 22:13). Usually this is interpreted as his being cast into hell in judgment. Certainly the language of "binding" (13:30), "outer darkness" (8:12), and "weeping and gnashing of teeth" (8:12) is judgment language in Matthew's Gospel, though the text does not mention hell here. It certainly denotes exclusion from the presence of the king/God and the broad community of those who enjoy his favor. God-at-work here means judgment, exclusion, and suffering. So in this way of reading, the allegory justifies the parable's strange turn and warns those enjoying the mercy of God in the wedding hall that responsibility and accountability for living faithfully come with the territory.

We can try and soften the king's action by saying that a life of faithlessness and lack of appreciation for God's mercy is itself a life of judgment. We bring it on ourselves with a lack of a lifestyle that honors the gracious invitation with faithful actions and gratefulness. Exclusion is then a consequence, but God is not its cause. There may well be some truth in this, but the parable is not so generous in its construction of the king/God. The king/God excludes the man by ordering his removal. This is God-at-work. Judgment extends even to those who enjoy the king's feast.

Or perhaps another detail helps. Clearly there is a big crowd of guests in the wedding hall; it is "filled with guests" (Matt 22:10). There is abundant food. There is an unlimited invitation. There is generous inclusion: "invite everyone you can find to the wedding banquet" (22:9). Yet out of all of these many, many guests, the king/God excludes only one guest in judgment. Only one. Love does carry the day—almost! (Oh but we can't forget the whole group of excluded leaders where the judgment seems more severe!).

But that's the discomforting piece. The parable shows God's grace to be abundant but limited. It does not stretch far enough to embrace everyone. The exclusion of even one guest is disconcerting. Perhaps the one rejected guy represents a whole group of folks? Or, reframing it, perhaps there is some encouragement in the way the parable's ending constructs the balance between judgment and mercy. Only one person excluded. Much more mercy than judgment is evident.

Or so it seems. Yet verse 14 may throw even this nice ending out of balance by seeming to reverse it. "Many are called, but few are chosen." The sequence here is not good. The parable's ending has shown the reverse with many chosen and a very few—one person—unworthy. Nevertheless this statement as the parable's final word does not produce an optimistic ending. Judgment and rejection, not love and inclusion, seem to express the parable's final construction of the dominant way of God-at-work.

In its construction of God, the parable has wobbled between grace (Matt 22:1-6), violent judgment (22:7), grace (22:8-10), judgment (22:12-13), grace (just one person, 22:11), and judgment (22:14). Or to use other words, the parable has swayed back and forth between mercy and harshness, between an inclusive and welcoming God and an excluding and rejecting God.

Its final word seems to emphasize judgment, but the king's repeated efforts to reach out and invite guests indicate determined and active inclusion. God-at-work is constructed in an ambivalent way.

Questions for Reflection/Discussion

1. Review the ways in which the king/God acts like a violent imperial tyrant in the parable.

2. Compare Matthew's parable with the version of the parable in Luke 14:16-24. What details are different? Note that Luke's version does not include a verse like Matthew 22:7 expressing the king's violent destruction of the city. What difference does this omission make to the presentation of God in Luke's version? Pay attention also to the context of Luke 14:1-15. How does it differ from the sequence of parables in Matthew 21:28-46 and what contribution does it make to the construction of God in the parable?

3. Basic to the parable is the king's provision of a wedding feast. The Bible uses the picture of inviting people to a banquet in different ways. Read, for example, Isaiah 25:5-10a for its presentation of God. In Proverbs 9:1-6, the female figure of wisdom sends out her servants/slaves to invite people to her feast:

    > Wisdom has built her house, she has hewn her seven pillars. She has slaughtered her animals, mixed her wine, set her table. She has sent out her servant girls; she calls from the highest places in the town, "You that are simple, turn in here!" To those without sense

she says, "Come, eat of my bread and drink of the wine I have mixed. Lay aside immaturity, and live, and walk in the way of insight." (Prov 9:1-6)

Lady Wisdom, as she is known, is presented as an image of God-at-work in the world. Compare the presentation of Wisdom's approach in this passage (her style? her guests? her promises?) to the presentation of the king in the parable. What differences do you notice? Which image of God do you prefer and why? For some other images of God as a woman, you might consider John 1:12; 1 John 4:7; Luke 15:8-10; Deut 32:11-12, 18; Isa 42:13-15; 49:14-15; 66:13; Hos 11:3-4; 13:8.

4. One of the interesting features of Matthew's parable is that while the Son, Jesus, is identified in verse 2 as the reason for and focus of the wedding banquet, he does not feature again. The parable centers on God's actions. Compare this focus with the previous parable in Matthew 21:33-44 and with the presentation of the intimate relationship between God as Father and Jesus as Son in Matthew 11:25-27.

Further Reading

Warren Carter, *Matthew and the Margins: A Sociopolitical and Religious Reading* (Maryknoll, NY: Orbis Books, 2000), 432–39.

Cynthia Jarvis and Elizabeth Johnson, *Feasting on the Gospels: Matthew*, vol. 2, chapters 14–28 (Louisville: Westminster John Knox, 2013), 182–87.

Ulrich Luz, *Matthew 21–28* (Minneapolis: Fortress, 2005), 45–60.

Neil Richardson, *Who on Earth is God? Making Sense of the Bible* (London: Bloomsbury, 2014), 77–102.

Chapter 4

The Good News and Empire of God (Mark 1:1-15)

> *Read Mark 1:1-15 before reading this chapter. Then refer to it while you read the chapter.*

Mark's Gospel begins its narrative of Jesus's public activity in this way:

> Now after John was arrested, Jesus came to Galilee, proclaiming the good news of God, and saying, "The time is fulfilled, and the kingdom of God has come near; repent and believe in the good news." (Mark 1:14-15)

From the get-go, Jesus is talking about God. Two times. He announces "the good news of God" and "the kingdom of God." The Gospel narrative focuses on Jesus, but Jesus is God's PR man, an ad-man selling good news.

But is Jesus a trustworthy source of knowledge about God? Is he reliable?

Mark 1:1-14a answers "yes" by establishing seven credentials for Jesus's reliability. God provides the main reference for Jesus.

Jesus's first credential is that God commissions him as "Christ" (Mark 1:1). This word, the Greek version of "Messiah," literally means "anointed one." Anointing with oil, for example, commissioned a priest (Lev 6:22) or a king (2 Sam 5:3; Ps 2:2) to carry out their God-given duties as a priest or a king. Subsequently, some Jewish folks expected different kinds of special "anointed ones" who would establish God's purposes on earth.[1] Verse 1 introduces Jesus as one whom God has commissioned to act on God's behalf.

Jesus's second credential is that he is "Son of God" (Mark 1:1). At this point in the Christian tradition, this term does not express Jesus's divinity as later Christian traditions involving the councils of Nicaea (325 CE) and Chalcedon (451 CE) affirm. In the Hebrew Bible, its meaning is much less exalted. There, the term refers to someone who is in special relation to God and acts as an agent or representative of God's will and purposes. So kings (Ps 2:7), Israel (Hosea 11:1), angels (Job 38:7), and righteous folks (Wis 2:18) are designated "sons" or children of God who carry out God's purposes. No one ever accused these folks of being divine. Jesus is such a person. Interestingly, the same language is used to identify Roman emperors, for whom the term especially designates their great power.

Jesus's third and fourth credentials come from the testimony of two important prophets, Isaiah and John the Baptist (Mark 1:2-3). The scriptures from Isaiah (with an assist from Malachi) are cited to declare John the Baptist's role to prepare the way for Jesus, calling people to be purified from sins. Jesus is located in the line of God's authorized spokespeople.

The fifth credential emerges in Jesus's baptism. The baptism is a mystical visionary scene, an occasion in which God speaks directly from heaven to Jesus: "You are my Son, the Beloved; with you I am well pleased" (Mark 1:11). The repetition of "Son of God" from verse 1 underscores the importance of Jesus's identity as God's agent. The designation "my Beloved" and expression of divine pleasure indicate not only divine favor but also the special and intimate relationship between God and Jesus. Jesus is presented as a trustworthy, God-approved source of knowledge about God.

Jesus's sixth credential (Mark 1:12-13) is quite different, comprising a practical test of being tempted by Satan. In these verses, we enter a strange world of spirits, angels, the devil, and wild beasts. Just how Jesus is tempted is not clear. Matthew and Luke's Gospels elaborate the scene with the temptation comprising a three-fold contest over Jesus's sonship or agency. Will Jesus be faithful to his identity as God's agent or will he take directions from the devil and become the devil's agent (Matt 4:1-11; Luke

4:1-13)? Jesus rejects the devil's threefold challenge and demonstrates his loyalty to God. He is an attested agent of God.

And his seventh credential confirms this loyalty. Verse 14a refers to the arrest of John the Baptist. No details of this arrest are provided here, and we will have to read on to 6:14-29 to find out about John's arrest and death by the rulers Herod and his wife Herodias. What is crucial is that Jesus is aligned with John (John baptized him) and John has risked his life in being faithful to the prophetic role God has commissioned him to carry out. There is a clear and present political danger to this sort of talk about God. Yet Jesus is not intimidated. Bravely and faithfully, he carries out his commission, true to his identity as God's anointed one and agent.

Seven credentials—quite a resumé and list of references. They establish Jesus as a faithful and reliable spokesperson for and representative of God. What does Jesus say about God-at-work?

Gospel of God

First, Jesus proclaims the "gospel of God" (Mark 1:14b). We think of this term *gospel* as a religious and Christian word that names the first four writings in the NT, the Gospels of Matthew, Mark, Luke, and John, or refers to the gospel of Jesus Christ. But here it concerns God. The term literally means "good news" or "good tidings" and its uses, outside Christian uses, say something about what God might be doing.

In the ancient world, it had a range of meanings. Several meanings are evident in a witty anecdote that mocks the crazy emperor Nero. Nero entered the competitions at the festival of Olympia in the categories of actor and performer on the harp. Naturally he won; no judge would be stupid enough not to declare an unstable emperor the winner! Nero sent out messengers to announce the "good news" of his victories and instruct residents to offer sacrifices and hymns of celebration. But some towns and villages had never heard of the Olympia festival and its competitions for acting and performing. When they heard about Nero's victories, they mistakenly understood the good news to be that Nero had won a military victory and that he had taken captives from a people called Olympians![2]

The term commonly designated victory in battle,[3] but it could refer to other kinds of good news (birth of a baby, a marriage). In a famous inscription from the city of Priene in Turkey, the term celebrates the good news of the birthday of the emperor Augustus, his coming of age, his accomplishments as savior in ending the civil war, his accession as emperor, and his numerous benefactions to his subjects.

The term *gospel* is also used in the Hebrew Bible. The good news involves God rescuing the psalmist from unspecified difficult circumstances (Ps 40:9) or delivering people in battle (Ps 68:11-12). Especially important is the good news/tidings that God delivers the people from exile in Babylon and from subjugation to their rule:

> Get you up to a high mountain, O Zion, herald of *good tidings*; lift up your voice with strength, O Jerusalem, herald of *good tidings* . . . say to the cities of Judah, "Here is your God!" See, the Lord GOD comes with might, and his arm rules for him. (Isa 40:9-10)

The good news comes by a

> messenger who announces peace, who brings *good news*, who announces salvation, who says to Zion, "Your God reigns." . . . for in plain sight they see the return of the LORD to Zion. Break forth together into singing, you ruins of Jerusalem; for the LORD has comforted his people, he has redeemed Jerusalem . . . and all the ends of the earth shall see the salvation of our God. (Isa 52:6-10)

Here the good news comprises God delivering the people from Babylonian power, using the victorious Persians to return them to their land, and establishing God's reign in their midst. And there is further good news. God "brings good news to the oppressed" (Isa 61:1).

What is the "good news of God" that Jesus proclaims in Mark 1:14? The little word *of* that joins "good news" and "God" indicates that the good news both comes from God and is about God. But what exactly is it? What are the good things that God is doing? The references from the Hebrew Bible suggest acts of deliverance, assertions of God's rule, victory over an imperial power like Rome. But for Mark's Gospel? At this point we don't know. We have to read on in the Gospel.

Mark 1:15: The Kingdom of God Has Come Near

Providing some clarification is Jesus's second announcement about God: "the kingdom of God has come near" (Mark 1:15). Again the phrase is difficult to understand. One problem concerns how to translate the word *kingdom*. The choice of different English words constructs different images of God.

For us, the term *kingdom* is antiquated and unreal. It suggests fairy tales or video games of damsels in distress, dragons, castles, and knights in armor on white horses. However we think about God, constructing fairy-tale images of God does not help.

Second, the language of *kingdom* presents a very masculine or patriarchal image of God. Kingdoms have kings who exercise great power over their subjects. In one sense, this image appropriately represents the Hebrew Bible tradition that presents God as king in ruling over and ordering human history and nations (Exod 15:11-13; Pss 95–100), in anticipation of the day when God establishes this rule in full (Mic 2:12-13; Dan 7:11-14; Zeph 3:14-20). On one hand, such an image of overwhelming power is not very inviting, and on the other hand, often in our chaotic and disordered world, God's rule does not seem visible or evident. The image claims something that often does not seem true.

Third, the presentation of a king ruling over others to describe God's activity in the world replicates an imperial "ruling over" model. This noun, sometimes translated *kingdom* and sometimes as *reign*, is used in biblical literatures to refer to empires such as the empires of Babylon, Medea, Persia, and Alexander's Macedonia (Dan 2:37-45). It is also used for the Roman Empire, the current ruling power in Mark's world (Josephus, *JW* 5.409). The rulers of these empires are tyrants who express their political rule in very tangible and harsh terms—represented by soldiers, taxes, slaves, and governors. We could, then, translate this phrase "the empire of God."

Yet the **Red flag** is waving. Such a translation presents God in a decidedly negative way. To translate the phrase as "the empire of God" constructs God in terms of domination, oppression, forced compliance, and punishment for disobedience. The translation suggests God mimics imperial practices and attributes the things of Caesar to God. These practices include violence, the unquestioning assertion of the divine will over nations and peoples, and punitive destruction for the resistant. And it claims at the same time, as all empires claim, that God's empire is good, just, and merciful.

Many find the terms *kingdom* and *empire* unsatisfactory because they emphasize God's power and violate human agency in requiring a submissive and unquestioning pose. Women have especially experienced these constructions negatively because they inscribe dominating male power. Others find such a harsh presentation of God to be off-putting.

Yet, as strange as it may seem, there is something "attention-getting" about the term "empire." It alerts us to the fact that God's rule is not just about individuals, or spiritual matters, or human hearts. God's rule is not just private. It is also about politics and about challenging destructive rulers, contesting their unfair socioeconomic practices, and negating their ideologies that claim divine sanction for unjust structures and exploitative practices. It is about God-at-work changing the structures and practices of the world in order to bless all people.

Other translations for the noun *kingdom* have been suggested. The term *kin-dom* suggests transformed relationships and a new community. Others have preferred to stay with *kingdom* or a synonym such as *realm* because they emphasize a place where God's activity and presence are encountered. Kingdoms have boundaries and borders; people "enter into" such a space and find God there in God's own space (Mark 9:47). But where is this elusive place?

Others have rejected this static sense, preferring a more active or dynamic sense with language of God's "rule" or "reign." This language constructs God-at-work actively among people but it does not specify how.

The phrase "kingdom/empire/reign/rule of God," then, raises some difficult questions about how to translate it and the images of God it constructs. We can recognize some overlap with the term "the good news of God," which also centered on God's reign or rule. But still, the language is vague. Can we gain any clarity as to what Jesus is saying about God-at-work?

Jesus's immediate words in Mark 1:14-15 help a little. He says that this kingdom/empire/reign/rule of God "has come near." This verb, "has come near," denotes a sense of time. Strangely, it is ambiguous about time, embracing both arrival and nearness, present and future dimensions. God is at work now but also in the future. Subsequent references in the Gospel bear this out. God's reign/empire/kingdom is both present in part already (4:11; 10:14-15, 23-25), but not yet in full until some point in the future when Jesus will establish it fully (9:1; 13:24-27; 15:43). But what exactly does it look like?

Jesus's next words show that it has a profound effect on people's lives. Jesus calls his hearers to respond to his proclamation about God-at-work. They are to "repent" or undergo a "change of mind," to change perspective and reflect different priorities and actions that express the good news of divine rule. To do so involves believing in, or better, committing themselves to, or being faithful to, or trusting this good news of God. The language of "believing/faith" is imperial language whereby subjugated peoples pledged loyalty and displayed faithfulness to Rome in order to become Rome's allies and subject to Rome's faithfulness.[4] Commitment to Jesus's proclamations about God involves, then, an alternative subjugation and loyalty to God. But exactly what is God doing? What is the good news of God? What does God's rule/reign/kingdom/empire look like? How is God-at-work?

To find out, we must read on and see how Jesus manifests God-at-work in his activity in Galilee.

Reading On: God-at-Work

Immediately in the next dramatic and cryptic scene, God-at-work is constructed as disruptive and reorienting (Mark 1:16-20). Jesus calls four fishermen to follow him, and strikingly, they respond immediately. God-at-work invades and disrupts their daily lives, work, and families. We are not told what Zebedee said as his family and workforce left and walked along the beach with Jesus (1:20)! Some words you can't print in the Bible! Jesus gives their lives a different focus and priority. They gain a new identity and mission to "fish for people." God's reign overrules and reorients their whole existence to participate in God's purposes. Strikingly, the "good news of God" is that God-at-work recruits and forms partnerships with people to share in God's purposes and reign.

This scene recurs in Mark 2:13-14 when Jesus summons Levi the tax collector to follow him. Tax collectors were no one's favorite people. There were three strikes against them. They collected taxes, which many folks didn't like to pay. They collected them for the Romans who occupied Galilee, so they were viewed as disloyal traitors for cooperating with the occupying power. And they were commonly thought to be thieves who collected more than they should. Jesus's opponents, the scribes of the Pharisees, disparage them as "sinners." This polemical term labels people who have fallen out of favor even with God! Jesus contradicts their verdict. His calling of Levi and dinner with him and his other tax-collecting mates show that God's good news and rule extend to any and everybody.

By Mark 3:13-19, Jesus has assembled a community of at least twelve male followers who have embraced and been embraced by God's rule. Jesus treats them as partners in proclaiming the good news and casting out demons. In chapter 6, he again entrusts them with a mission of exorcisms and healing (6:7-13). But—**Red-flag alert**—why no women?

Jesus's next action again displays God's good rule at work. He encounters a man who has convulsions caused by an "unclean spirit" or demon and casts it out (Mark 1:21-28). This exorcism represents a major conflict in the Gospel. The Gospel, like other writings of its time, claims that one of the reasons that the world is out of joint, that things are not as they should be, is that the devil or Satan promotes its own kingdom or rule (3:22-29). The devil works through agents (demons or evil spirits) to oppose God's purposes (1:12-13) and create havoc in people's lives. Jesus's exorcisms assert God's reign or power over Satan, repair the damage, and establish new lives (5:1-20; 7:24-30). This is the good news of God-at-work.

A further display of God's rule and good news follows (Mark 1:29-34). In addition to exorcisms, Jesus transforms the lives of sick people with healings. The Gospel is full of sick people, and Jesus repeatedly heals

> **The Testament of Solomon**
>
> A document called the *Testament of Solomon* shows this pervasive understanding that demons created havoc in human lives, relationships, and society. The demons have names and responsibilities for particular human problems. Many demons cause diseases in particular parts of the body: for example, headaches; damage to eyes, throats, and ears; paralysis of limbs; colic of the bowels; kidney pains; problems with tendons; chills and shivering; numbness; convulsions; fevers; pains in the heart and ribs; diarrhea and hemorrhoids; and insomnia. Other demons cause divisions in families, disputes among people, jealousies and squabbles, demolition of houses, wars and battles, factions and strife, and raise up and depose tyrants and kings (selections from chapters 8 and 18).

them (1:40-45; 2:1-12; 3:7-12; 6:53-56). Why are there so many sick folks?

The explanation lies in the impact of the structures of the Roman Empire. Elites in the empire controlled the production and distribution of food so food supplies followed lines of power. Powerful figures ate well but common folks often struggled for access to adequate nutrition. As a result, diseases from deficient nutrition and from vulnerability to contagion were rife. Jesus's healings enact God's good news in repairing this damage and giving folks new lives. The prophet Isaiah envisioned the establishment of God's reign as providing "for all peoples a feast of rich food" (Isa 25:5-10b). Jesus reflects and anticipates this glorious feast by providing several extravagant meals for crowds of more than five thousand and four thousand (Mark 6:30-44; 8:1-10).

But also, the scriptures talk of physical healing and wholeness as a sign of God establishing God's reign. So Isaiah announces, "Here is your God. . . . He will come and save you. Then the eyes of the blind shall be opened, and the ears of the deaf unstopped; then the lame shall leap like a deer, and the tongue of the speechless sing for joy" (Isa 35:4-6). Jesus's healings are not just displays of razzle-dazzle power. Rather, he enacts the good news of God that creates new lives in ruling over diseases. He heals the blind (Mark 8:22-25; 10:46-52), deaf (Mark 7:32-37; 9:25), paralyzed

(Mark 2:1-12), speechless (Mark 7:32-37), a man with a withered or dried up hand (a terrible impediment in a society relying on manual labor; Mark 3:1-6), and a woman with an unstoppable hemorrhage; he even raises a dead girl back to life (Mark 5:21-48). And as part of the partnership with the good news of God-at-work that Jesus has called his followers into, he sends them out to continue this same work of casting out demons (Mark 3:15; 6:7) and healing the sick (Mark 6:13). These actions establish God's reign at work among people.

Finally, Jesus continues to proclaim the good news of God and reign/empire/kingdom of God with words. He goes around Galilee teaching (Mark 1:21-22; 2:13; 6:2) and proclaiming (1:38-39). He tells parables that explain what "the kingdom of God is like." The parable of the sower shows that God's reign is not automatically effective; various circumstances thwart God's work (4:3-9). Its presence is mysterious and difficult to discern (4:10-12). It is like a seed that a sower sows and which grows even though the sower does not know how—eventually and certainly it comes to completion or maturity (4:26-29). It is like a mustard seed, very small and inconsequential in the present, invisible (is anything happening under the ground?), yet inevitably the small seed becomes a big shrub; its growth is underway (it takes time; 4:30-32). The parables explain God-at-work in the present but provide assurance of God's present and future activity. Jesus's words elaborate the good news of God and God's reign.

The "good news of God" and "kingdom of God" are phrases, then, that depict God-at-work among humans, sometimes mysteriously and invisibly in the midst of Rome's empire yet certainly and inevitably. God is constructed as performing transformations through Jesus that express God's life-giving, loving, powerful, disruptive favor. God acts for human good, even though the image of God's kingdom or empire is masculine, kingly, and imperial and thereby not unambiguously positive as we have noted. And, of course, the pervasive brokenness and suffering in our world raises the question of the power, extent, and effectiveness of God-at-work in our world.

Questions for Reflection/Discussion

1. Psalms 95–99 celebrate God's rule as king over the earth as something already established but yet to be realized fully. Read several of these Psalms and describe God's reign. What continuities do you see with Jesus's actions?

2. The phrase "the gospel" or "good news of God" appears elsewhere in the NT in Romans 1:1. Read Romans 1:1-6; what does it say about God's good news and how does this compare with Mark's presentation?

3. Discuss the different translation options for the word "kingdom." What different constructions of God result? Which ones do you find acceptable and which ones are disturbing?

4. Jesus demonstrates the "good news of God" and the "kingdom of God" in various actions, both in the present and in the future (Mark 8:38–9:1; 13:24-27). Do you see the good news of God and the kingdom of God at work in our world? If so, where?

Further Reading

Clifton Black, *Mark* (Nashville: Abingdon, 2011), 64–68.

William Placher, *Mark* (Louisville: Westminster John Knox, 2010), 30–35.

Chapter 5

My God, My God, Why Have You Forsaken Me? (Mark 15:34)

> Read Mark 15:34 before reading this chapter. Then refer to it while you read the chapter.

As Jesus dies on the cross, he cries out to God, "My God, My God, why have you forsaken me?" His cry expresses his sense that God has abandoned him. It echoes across the centuries, resonating with every person who in situations of pain, danger, despair, loss, desperation, and death has cried out for God's saving intervention—only to be met, so it seems, with no response, with divine silence, passivity, impotence, indifference. Across the millennia, various figures such as John of the Cross and Mother Teresa have experienced this mysterious and terribly painful, dark night of the soul, this eclipse of God, God-forsakenness.

Mark's Gospel begins with God declaring Jesus to be God's beloved son (1:11). **Red-flag alert**—what sort of God abandons his beloved son in the moment of death, especially a death on a cross that the Jewish historian Josephus calls "the most pitiable of deaths"? How do we understand this most troubling construction of God?

The Death of Jesus

Mark's Gospel presents Jesus's death as multilayered, involving a number of players:

- The Pharisees went out and immediately conspired with the Herodians against him, how to destroy him. (Mark 3:6)

- They were . . . going up to Jerusalem . . . [Jesus] took the twelve aside again and began to tell them what was to happen to him, saying, "See, we are going up to Jerusalem, and the Son of Man will be handed over to the chief priests and the scribes, and . . . to the Gentiles . . . ; they will . . . kill him." (10:32-34)

- And when the chief priests and the scribes heard it, they kept looking for a way to kill him. (11:18)

- [An unnamed woman] "has done what she could; she has anointed my body beforehand for its burial. Truly I tell you, wherever the good news is proclaimed in the whole world, what she has done will be told in remembrance of her." (14:8-9)

- Then Judas Iscariot, who was one of the twelve, went to the chief priests in order to betray him to them . . . they were greatly pleased and promised to give him money. (14:10-11)

- And Jesus said to [the disciples], "You will all become deserters" . . . All of them deserted him and fled. . . . But [Peter] began to curse, and he swore an oath, "I do not know this man you are talking about." At that moment, the cock crowed for the second time. Then Peter remembered that Jesus had said to him, "Before the cock crows twice, you will deny me three times." And he broke down and wept. (14:27, 50, 71-72)

- As soon as it was morning, the chief priests held a consultation with the elders and scribes and the whole council. They bound Jesus, led him away, and handed him over to Pilate . . . [who] handed him over to be crucified. (15:1, 15)

- When the Sabbath was over, Mary Magdalene, Mary the mother of James, and Salome bought spices, so that they might go and anoint him [Jesus]. (16:1)

My God, My God, Why Have You Forsaken Me? (Mark 15:34)

It's quite a cast: political opponents, Jesus journeying to Jerusalem and not running away, a woman lovingly recognizing his imminent death, a traitorous disciple, frightened and big-talking disciples cowered into betrayal, a tough Roman governor and his allies, women lovingly preparing his body for burial. All play their parts.

But another cast member is missing from this list. What is God's role in Jesus's death? Jesus cries out to God, mysteriously addressing God as though God were present yet lamenting God's absence, complaining to God as though God were present that God has abandoned him. The Gospel story shows Jesus expecting God's involvement in his death. What does God—and what sort of God—have to do with Jesus's death?

God the Puppet Master?

Through the first eight chapters of Mark, Jesus demonstrates the "good news of God" and "the kingdom/reign/rule/empire of God" in his transformative actions of creating some sort of community, healing the sick, casting out demons, feeding the hungry, and explaining God's reign. But halfway through the Gospel comes a startling announcement. The narrator tells us that Jesus

> began to teach them that the Son of Man must undergo great suffering, and be rejected by the elders, the chief priests, and the scribes, and be killed, and after three days rise again. He said all this quite openly. (Mark 8:31-32)

The strange term *Son of Man*, which could also be translated "child of humanity" or "Human One," is a Bible phrase. It occurs in several different contexts in the Hebrew Bible. In Ezekiel, God addresses the prophet Ezekiel by this term; it's translated "mortal" (which is a whole lot nicer than "hey you!"):

> He said to me: O mortal, stand up on your feet, and I will speak with you. (Ezek 2:1; also 3:1)

In addressing the prophet with this term, *Son of Man* or *mortal*, God instructs Ezekiel on what to do. The term identifies the prophet as God's messenger or spokesperson.

The same term appears with a very different meaning in a very different context in Daniel 7. Here the scene is international and cosmic. The Son of Man is a heavenly figure. In a vision, he appears before God after four powerful beasts—representing the Babylonian, Medean, Persian, and Macedonian/Greek empires—have appeared and vanished (Dan 7:13-14). God gives this Son of Man figure great power, appointing him an agent of God's rule with "dominion and glory and kingship" that will never end. God makes him God's representative in exercising God's rule over all people who are to serve him. This agent of God's rule seems human-like and heavenly, individual (Dan 7:13) and corporate (Dan 7:18, 27).

These two uses of the term *Son of Man* in Ezekiel (human) and in Daniel (heavenly) seem very different. But they have one thing in common. In both instances, the term designates a figure who acts on behalf of God. In both instances, the term refers to someone who carries out God's purposes and will.

By using this term for Jesus, Mark's Gospel emphasizes that Jesus does God's will and purposes. And here in 8:31, that means Jesus undergoes great suffering and death. This use of the term indicates that God wills Jesus's death.

Another word in 8:31 points in this same direction. Jesus teaches his disciples that he as Son of Man *must* undergo great suffering and die in Jerusalem at the hands of the Jewish and Gentile leaders. Why the verb *must*? Peter disagrees in verse 32 that such a terrible thing could happen to Jesus, but Jesus harshly rebukes him by telling him he is opposing "divine things" and allied with Satan against God's purposes! What Jesus *must* do—experience a terrible death—clearly seems to be God's will. He *must* die because God says so.

Several more times in the subsequent chapters Jesus repeats himself, saying he is to die in Jerusalem:

- for he was teaching his disciples, saying to them, "The Son of Man is to be betrayed into human hands, and they will kill him, and three days after being killed, he will rise again." But they did not understand what he was saying and they were afraid to ask him. (Mark 9:31-32)

- See, we are going up to Jerusalem, and the Son of Man will be handed over to the chief priests and the scribes, and they will condemn him to death; then they will hand him over to the Gentiles. They will mock him, and spit upon him, and flog him, and kill him. (Mark 10:33-34)

The repetition underscores the importance of the event and the perspective that as God's agent Jesus dies, and this is God's will. Jesus's death is, according to this reading of these verses, God's predestined plan.

The **Red flag** is waving. This construction of God sending God's beloved son to die is hard to understand and accept. The disciples certainly struggle to make sense of it (Mark 9:32) and Peter rejects it outright (8:32). Across the ages, numerous readers have found this image of God impossible to accept. It constructs God as a monster in killing his own son. It presents God as consigning this beloved son to a torturous death and makes God guilty of child abuse and murder.

Such a God hardly seems worthy of worship and trust. And such a God seems very much at odds with other biblical presentations of a loving and merciful God. As we have seen, Mark's Gospel begins by announcing the "good news of God."

Further, this presentation of Jesus's torturous death as prescribed by God suggests that God ordains suffering as a normal part of God's will. To struggle against suffering in everyday life, to seek to repair and heal the suffering that pervades our world—whether from violence or natural disasters or human conflict or unjust structures and practices—would then be to live against God's purposes! But in the first half of the Gospel, Jesus does precisely that, repairing and alleviating suffering in his healings, exorcisms, feedings, and formation of inclusive community. Jesus does not accept suffering passively as divinely ordained.

And further, to say that Jesus's death is predestined by God ignores human involvement in and responsibility for Jesus's death. Throughout the Gospel, Jesus was in conflict with the leaders of Jerusalem. They oversaw a society that benefitted themselves as the rich and powerful, at the expense of the poor and common folks. While they want to observe Sabbath by insisting on rest (which maintains the status quo), Jesus sees it as a day for doing good and saving lives, which he demonstrates in his healings (Mark 3:4). While they encourage people to give money to their power base, the temple, even if it causes hardship for elderly parents, Jesus rebukes them for failing to honor or care for those vulnerable elderly folks (7:9-13). While they turn the temple into a money-making enterprise, Jesus attacks them for not administering a house for prayer (11:15-19). They fear his popularity with the crowds (11:18). He condemns them for not being faithful in looking after the "vineyard" (Israel) God has entrusted to them (12:1-12). They, along with the Roman governor Pilate, decide that such a destabilizing critic must die.

Divinely Predestined or Political Inevitability?

So here's the key question: what does "must" mean? Why "must" Jesus die? It is one thing to say that suffering can be embraced within the purposes of God and that God might be present in its midst and even work some good in it and from it. It is, though, quite another thing to say that God *causes* suffering and death.

Is Jesus's death predestined by God as a divine necessity? Or is his death an inevitable and necessary political consequence of his activity that conflicts with and challenges the interests of the powerful leaders?

While interpreters have often preferred divine predestination, the Gospel of Mark seems to point instead to political inevitability. Jesus reinterprets the significance of the Sabbath so the Pharisees and Herodians decide he must die (3:1-6). Jesus challenges the temple leaders and they decide he must die (11:18). He speaks against the temple and they plan to put him to death (14:1-2). Political inevitability means removing a rival and rebel.

Regularly in the biblical story, God's agents suffer as a result of political challenges and collisions. Moses demands that Pharaoh set the people free, and Pharaoh tries to kill him and his people (Exod 14). The prophet Elijah calls King Ahab and Queen Jezebel to repent and abandon their idolatrous ways, and he has to flee for his life (1 Kgs 19). John the Baptist confronts Herod Antipas for his illicit marriage to Herodias, the wife of Herod's brother Philip, and in a bizarre but deadly scene, John loses his head (Mark 6:14-29). Jesus has been faithful to his identity as God's agent and Son and loses his life.

In losing his life, Jesus experiences rejection and pain. Rejecting Jesus as God's agent is, of course, to reject God. Might we imagine that God suffers and grieves in such circumstances also? The God of the Bible is no stranger to suffering and hardship. The people wander in the wilderness but God does not abandon them. God travels with them, present in their midst through a pillar of cloud by day and a pillar of fire by night (Exod 13). When the Babylonians send the nation's leaders into exile after destroying Jerusalem in 587 BCE, Ezekiel announces some stunning good news. God has gone into exile with the people (Ezek 1)! When God seems to have abandoned the people, God is present and suffers in their midst.

The Rest of the Story

But there is more to the story. Jesus does not avoid conflict with Jerusalem's power group. He does not run away. He is not a victim taken by surprise. He cooperates. He goes willingly to Jerusalem, the center of their power. And he declares that he gives "his life a ransom for many" (Mark 10:45). What does it mean to give his life a ransom for many? What sort of God inspires people to give away their lives, to become martyrs?

To "ransom" someone is to set them free. In the ancient world, prisoners of war and slaves were ransomed when someone paid a ransom to set them free. The word is used in the biblical tradition to refer to God's action of ransoming or setting free the Israelites from slavery in Egypt (Deut 7:8) and from captivity in Babylon (Isa 43:1). God does not pay a price to anyone to accomplish this freedom. God acts powerfully to accomplish it.

Jesus talks, then, about giving his life as "a ransom for many." The word *for* signifies that his death has an effect on or benefits others. Just how this happens the Gospel does not say. There is no indication that Mark's Gospel understands Jesus to be a sacrifice acceptable to God that takes away the sin of the world. Nor is there any indication that Jesus is a ransom God has paid to the devil to free humans from sin. How does Jesus's death benefit others?

Throughout, Jesus has been in conflict with the Jerusalem and Roman leaders. His death is a moral confrontation with their oppressive power. It shows the destructiveness of their power in protecting their own interests. It shows the lengths to which they will go to resist God's purposes and agent. Jesus dies absorbing their violence and experiencing the full cruelty and destructiveness of their actions. God does not save him and Jesus dies feeling abandoned by God and experiencing God-forsakenness.

Where is the setting free? Where is the benefit for others?

Quoting Psalm 22

Jesus's cry from the cross ("My God, my God . . .") is, in fact, a quotation from a psalm. It is the opening line of Psalm 22, which is known as a lament psalm. Lament psalms describe a particular form of difficult human experience and a surprising encounter with God. Usually the psalmist is in great trouble and suffering and initially finds no help from God.

In Psalm 22, the psalmist complains that God does not help him and ignores his groaning or whining (Ps 22:1). This neglect is made worse, it seems, because in the past God has responded to the cries of God's people and even to the psalmist's appeals for help (Ps 22:3-5, 9-11). But now, even though the psalmist looks for God's intervention, God seems passive, unresponsive, and uncaring. The psalmist's troubles involve people who scorn, despise, and mock him, taunting him with the suggestion that if God "delighted" in him he would not be experiencing suffering (Ps 22:6-8). The identity of these tormentors or enemies is not specified. They suggest that the psalmist's suffering indicates God's displeasure or punishment. Under these pressures, the psalmist's health deteriorates even to the point of death (Ps 22:14-15). He accuses God, "You lay me in the dust of death." He describes his experience of his enemies in animal images: surrounded by bulls, threatened by roaring lions, and endangered by wild oxen. His enemies gloat over him and divide his clothing (Ps 22:16-18). "My God, my God, why have you forsaken me?"

Just when things cannot get any worse, suddenly, somehow, God rescues him (Ps 22:22b). The psalmist does not describe how this happens or even what comprises his rescue. But something happens and he celebrates that God "did not despise or abhor" his affliction, that God "did not hide his face from me but heard when I cried to him" (Ps 22:24). As much as the psalm laments God's absence, it also celebrates God's powerful presence. Clearly he is singing from a very different hymn sheet in the last nine or so verses of the psalm than in the first twenty!

The psalm sets out a paradoxical spirituality of absence and presence, of apparent abandonment yet divine intervention. The person who knows God is absent in his suffering surprisingly finds God present, precisely there in the midst of his suffering. The person who seems to have been abandoned by God in suffering and distress surprisingly finds rescue and relief from God's presence in the midst of that suffering. The person who seems to be punished by God is favored and vindicated by God. God is seen to have entered into this suffering and its vulnerability, to be present even when God seems absent, and to suffer with the apparently abandoned one.

None of these is an easy cliché. They are hard-won, time-tested affirmations that emerge from human suffering.

In addition to this cry of abandonment, Mark's narrative of Jesus's death includes other aspects from this psalm. Jesus, too, is surrounded by enemies (Mark 14:10-11, 43-65), mocked (15:16-20), and trapped by a company of evildoers (15:27-32). His enemies shake their heads at him and divide his clothing (15:24, 29). Jesus fully experiences this human and divine abandonment. Yet neither Psalm 22 nor Mark's narrative ends there.

Like the psalmist, Jesus experiences God's deliverance—not from death but in resurrection (Mark 16). Jesus has declared previously that not only must he suffer and die but also that God would raise him from the dead (Mark 8:31). Jesus's enemies cannot keep him dead. God's power and presence are not confined by nor absent from his death. God remains faithful to Jesus even through and after his death when God seems to have abandoned him. God surprisingly works outside and beyond human limits and perceptions.

The notion of resurrection emerged in Israel's thinking in a context of political tyranny and martyrdoms under the Seleucid ruler and tyrant

Antiochus Epiphanes in the second century BCE. Antiochus had prohibited observance of Israel's distinctive practices like circumcision, festivals, and food purity laws. Seven brothers refused Antiochus's order to eat pig meat and, according to 2 Maccabees 7, Antiochus set about torturing them into submission. He mutilates their bodies by cutting off their tongues, hands, and feet and scalping them. But they die utterly confident that God will raise them from the dead, restore their bodies to wholeness, and reunite them with each other and their mother.

Resurrection was understood to belong to the new age in which God's purposes would be established in full over all tyranny and oppression. It was a sign that nothing could obstruct the establishment of God's purposes. By giving his life as a ransom for many, Jesus's death creates the opportunity for God to display resurrecting power, justice, and presence in repairing the damage of tyrants and setting up God's reign.

This way of thinking affirmed God's power, presence, and good purposes even when it seemed that tyrants, evildoers, and every form of sin and destruction reigned supreme among humans. Even if tyrants seemed to be indestructible in the present, it did not mean that God was faithless, passive, absent, or impotent. It did not mean God was too weak or unmoved by human suffering. Rather it affirmed that God's power was present in the midst of such suffering, that God, too, knew the pain of suffering and death, and that God's commitment to justice and saving power was unshakeable.

God's apparent absence and presence create a paradox as God enters fully and freely into human suffering and works with God's agents to accomplish God's life-giving purposes—even when God seems absent.

Questions for Reflection/Discussion

1. In the Apocrypha, read about Antiochus Epiphanes and the emergence of the understanding of resurrection. Start with 1 Maccabees 1, then 2 Maccabees 7 and the martyrdom of the seven brothers. What dynamics of divine presence and absence do you see?

My God, My God, Why Have You Forsaken Me? (Mark 15:34)

2. Various New Testament texts promise divine presence with God's people. Read Matthew 1:23; 18:19-20; 28:20; Revelation 21:1-5. How do you reconcile such promises with the experience of divine absence and abandonment?

3. There's an old bumper sticker that reads: "If you don't feel close to God, guess who moved?" The implication is that you, O faithless Mortal, abandoned God. In the light of Jesus's cry from the cross and the experience of Psalm 22, what might the psalmist and Jesus say in response to the bumper sticker?

Further Reading

Warren Carter and Amy-Jill Levine, *The New Testament: Methods and Meanings* (Nashville: Abingdon, 2013), 36–53.

Raquel St. Clair, *Call and Consequence: A Womanist Reading of Mark* (Minneapolis: Fortress, 2008).

Chapter 6

God and the Powerful and the Powerless (Luke 1:47-58; 6:20-26)

> *Read Luke 1:47-58; 6:20-26 before reading this chapter. Then refer to these passages while you read the chapter.*

In the late twentieth century, huge political changes took place in the world. In Europe, communist rule in Poland, Hungary, East Germany, Czechoslovakia, Bulgaria, and Albania collapsed. The Soviet Union comprising some dozen republics such as the Ukraine, Belarus, Estonia, Latvia, and Lithuania broke apart. So, too, did Yugoslavia.

In the 1990s in South Africa the practice of apartheid was abolished. Apartheid was a system of legally instituted racial segregation whereby the majority black and colored populations were oppressed with their movement, rights, and assembly severely restricted by the minority, ruling, white Afrikaner government. The world community had widely criticized the policy with economic and sporting boycotts exerting pressure for change.

In 2014, voters in Scotland rejected the proposition that Scotland should be a country independent of the United Kingdom. In 2015, the United States Supreme Court declared same-sex marriages legal. Supporters of the decision hailed it as "being on the right side of history" in its movement toward justice for all. Opponents saw it as a betrayal of God's purposes for marriage.

Various experts such as historians and political scientists identify a range of factors that account for each of these events. But what about theologians? Do they have a perspective to offer? Did God have anything to do with any of these events?

According to the two passages from Luke's Gospel we discuss in this chapter, the surprising answer is yes! These passages assert God-at-work in human history. God "has brought down the powerful from their thrones and lifted up the lowly" (1:52). In this construction, God has a political agenda and a socioeconomic bias toward empowering the poor and powerless.

Was God working for the political changes in Europe, South Africa, and the US? But what about that vote in Scotland? If God has a bias toward the poor, why are so many members of the human family still lacking basic necessities? And *if* we are among the world's privileged, the wealthy, the powerful, those of higher status, how do we respond to these texts' insistence that God has this bias? *And if* we are among the world's poor . . . ?

Luke 1:47-55: Mary's Song

In the first part of Mary's Song, Mary praises God for God's action in her conception of Jesus (Luke 1:47-49). The second part widens the focus to God's work in human history, praising God for God's "mercy is for those who fear him from generation to generation" (1:50-55). Let's start with Mary's experience.

Mary's celebration follows the angel Gabriel's stunning announcement on behalf of God. Gabriel announces that as a result of God's favor, Mary would conceive a child who would be God's son/agent and receive the throne of David (Luke 1:26-38). The angel's announcement comes true, Mary is pregnant, and the word of the Lord is shown to be an efficacious and secure means of initiating God's purposes among humans (1:38, 45). No matter how familiar the story is to us, we must not miss the scene's construction of God as interventionist, even invasionist, surprising, unpredictable, unconventional, powerful, life-giving, and effective.

Mary begins her hymn by naming God as her savior. The next couple of verses elaborate God's saving to comprise favoring the powerless and low-status Mary. She celebrates God's favor on her "lowliness" and identifies herself as God's "slave," readily obedient to God's will (Luke 1:48).

It's a little more complicated than that, of course. In fact, it's downright disturbing, a clear **Red-flag moment**. Mary doesn't have any choice in the matter (Luke 1:48)! She isn't asked for her consent! She doesn't give it! What we have named as God's intervention could be described as God's violation of Mary, God's slave.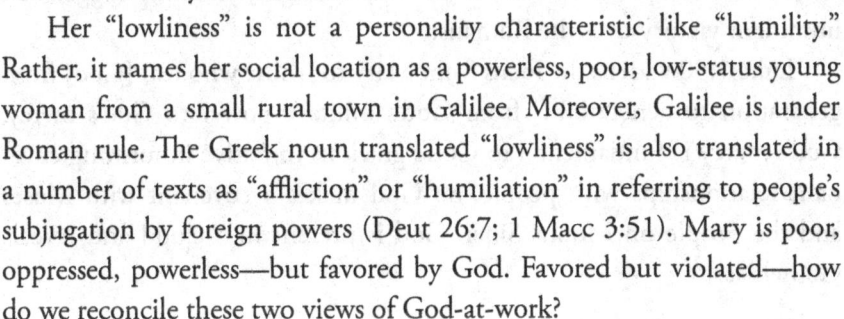

Her "lowliness" is not a personality characteristic like "humility." Rather, it names her social location as a powerless, poor, low-status young woman from a small rural town in Galilee. Moreover, Galilee is under Roman rule. The Greek noun translated "lowliness" is also translated in a number of texts as "affliction" or "humiliation" in referring to people's subjugation by foreign powers (Deut 26:7; 1 Macc 3:51). Mary is poor, oppressed, powerless—but favored by God. Favored but violated—how do we reconcile these two views of God-at-work?

At no point does the narrative say why she experiences God's favor (1:29-30). But one thing is clear: God exercises a socioeconomic bias in choosing a poor and powerless woman from a subjugated people to play a crucial role in God's purposes. God does not choose an elite, powerful, privileged, wealthy starlet.

Nor does the narrative say that God's favor makes things easy for Mary. Being an unwed pregnant woman did not conform to society's ideal cultural norms for young betrothed women. We can imagine gossips declaring *she* must have been unfaithful to her betrothed! Several texts express curses on unmarried pregnant women and their children:

> Her children will not take root, and her branches will not bear fruit. She will leave behind an accursed memory and her disgrace will never be blotted out. (Sir 23:25-26; also Wis Sol 3:16-19; 4:3-6)

But the hymn's attention falls on God, not Mary's challenges. God is constructed as coloring outside the lines. God runs with scissors. It is precisely among the powerless and the cursed, not the powerful and wealthy, that God is at work. Mary's personal circumstances, then, personify and represent the oppression of her people.

The image of God-at-work now changes from the Savior of the lowly to the "Mighty One." This image of God as the Mighty One moves beyond God's favor on the powerless and poor to God's actions on their behalf. Specifically, it depicts God as a Divine Warrior who goes to battle on behalf of God's people against their enemies. Psalm 24 describes the Lord as "strong and mighty, the LORD, mighty in battle" (Ps 24:8). Isaiah 10 celebrates the victories of this mighty God over the Egyptians and the Assyrians. Perhaps this emphasis on God as mighty in battle suggests an imminent victory over the Romans.

Luke 1:50 widens the focus from Mary to "those who fear [God] from generation to generation," from God's military power to God's mercy. God's mercy is fundamental to God's gracious initiative in forming covenant relationships with people. So God makes a covenant with Moses and the people on Mount Sinai. God is present in a cloud and reveals Godself as:

> The LORD! The LORD! a God merciful and gracious, slow to anger, and abounding in steadfast love and faithfulness, keeping steadfast love for the thousandth generation, forgiving iniquity and transgression and sin. (Exod 34:6-7)

God's mercy is synonymous here with God's graciousness and abundant, steadfast love. God is relentlessly faithful across thousands of generations. Even human faithlessness cannot subvert God's mercy because God forgives it and sets it aside. Mercy, then, is not just a characteristic of God. It is a power. Mercy is God-at-work.

God's merciful power-at-work is referred to as "strength with his arm" (Luke 1:51). This is an anthropomorphic presentation of God—which means God is presented in human terms. With a powerful arm, God accomplishes major actions. As the arm-wrestling world champion, God creates the world (Ps 89:12-13), frees the people from slavery in Egypt (Exod 6:1, 6), and protects them from other threatening nations (Deut 7:19).

God and the Powerful and the Powerless (Luke 1:47-58; 6:20-26)

Luke 1:51-53 elaborates three further acts of God's powerful mercy. In each action, God reverses current situations in which the proud, powerful, and rich are presented as enemies of God's good purposes. God's actions bring privileges and oppressions to an end in creating a different world.

In the first reversal, God "has scattered the proud in the thoughts of their hearts." The heart refers to the center of human willing, thinking, knowing, and deciding. The term *proud* could also be translated as "arrogant." The arrogant are those who resist God rather than welcome God's favor, as the lowly and powerless Mary does. So the scribes and Pharisees resist Jesus's declarations of forgiveness (Luke 5:21-22), his practice of fostering community that includes anyone (Luke 5:39-32), and his healing on a Sabbath (Luke 6:6-8; 14:1-4). Their arrogance means they do not prize what God prizes and cannot welcome God's son (Luke 16:14-15).

The second reversal is that God "has brought down the powerful from their thrones and lifted up the lowly (Luke 1:52). Various biblical passages attest God-at-work bringing low the powerful and exalting the powerless (1 Sam 2:7). So for example

> The Lord overthrows the thrones of rulers, and enthrones the lowly in their place. The Lord plucks up the roots of the nations, and plants the humble in their place. The Lord lays waste the lands of the nations. (Sir 10:14-16).

Other examples include God freeing the people from slavery in Egypt, David's victory over Goliath, the successful Maccabean revolt against the Seleucid tyrant Antiochus Epiphanes, and the gruesome death of Herod, who was struck down by an angel of the Lord for accepting the acclamation that he was a god and not a mortal and "was eaten by worms" (Acts 12:20-23). The primary example here of lifting up the lowly or powerless is the choice of Mary.

God's third socioeconomic reversal concerns the rich and the hungry. God fills the hungry and sends "the rich away empty" (Luke 1:53). To send someone away empty is a punishment because it deprives them of resources (Luke 20:10-11). So in Deuteronomy 15:13-14, if a master sets a slave free, "you shall not send him out empty-handed;" instead "provide [for him] liberally out of your flock, your threshing floor, and your wine press." The division between the rich and the poor and hungry was basic to the ancient world. The rich, some 2 or 3 percent of the population, enjoyed abundant resources and food, while the poor (comprising various levels of poverty) struggled for adequate nutrition. God's reversal effects a fundamental societal transformation. It does not glorify or romanticize poverty, but it envisions God-at-work for a world in which there is no poverty.

The song ends by reaffirming God-at-work previously with Israel, faithful to God's covenant promises. Abraham is specifically mentioned, recalling the promise that through him God would bless all the families of the earth. Does that "all" include the proud, the powerful, and the privileged?

The notion of the gods intervening in human and national affairs to effect a change of fortune was common in the ancient world. Odysseus in Homer's *Odyssey* frequently tells this story. But here's the challenge and a bunch of disturbing **Red-flag questions** for contemporary readers. Where in our world do we see God-at-work in the ways celebrated in Mary's song? Does God intervene in national and international affairs? Really? Some of us don't see signs of God's presence in our own lives, let alone among the nations. Does God act on behalf of the poor and empower us/them for better lives? If so why are there still so many poor folks? How do those who are rich and privileged respond to that bias? Does God act against the powerful and rich to punish them or to rehabilitate them for a world community marked by justice and equality? Does God act on God's own or does God partner with human agents and agencies in doing this work for justice? Is God-at-work?

Luke 6:20-23: Four Beatitudes

The Gospel of Luke returns several times to this theme of God's bias in favor of the poor and God's commitment to reverse the unjust structures and practices administered by the rich and powerful. This passage (6:20-26) features four beatitudes and four woes. Beatitudes are declarations. They declare God's blessings or God's favor. They identify and describe God-at-work, how and where and among whom God's favor is experienced and to what effect.

God and the Powerful and the Powerless (Luke 1:47-58; 6:20-26)

The first beatitude stunningly announces God's blessing on the poor. No one ever thinks the poor are blessed. Conventional wisdom says that the rich and powerful, the lucky and the smart, the well-connected and the privileged are blessed, not the poor. Who are these poor that God blesses?

Some say they are the spiritually poor, those who know their lives are empty without God and are open to God's presence. But Luke's previous chapters do not support this spiritual identification. Rather, they suggest that the poor whom God blesses are the literal poor, lacking material resources and options and societally marginalized, just like Mary. They are small-town folks from the poor village of Nazareth (4:16-30). They are the demon-possessed, the sick, those suffering with leprosy, the paralyzed, those with disabilities like a withered hand.

All of these are debilitating conditions that prevent folks from working and supporting themselves and their households, thereby consigning them to perpetual poverty. They are conditions that marginalize people, isolating them from others and from involvement in human community. They are situations that provoke hostility, prejudice, rejection, and judgment. They are situations that lack conventional markers of success and standing. They are situations that cause people to conclude that God's blessing rests on the wealthy and successful, not on the poor (Deut 28).

Jesus's first beatitude confronts such "conventional wisdom" to announce that God's blessing, God's reign, and the kingdom of God is found among poor folks. Unlike other kingdoms and empires where the powerful and wealthy elite occupy the privileged places and reap the benefits of power, these poor folks—of varying means and deprivations—occupy the central place in God's purposes. This is God-at-work, reversing current values, perspectives, and structures of the Roman Empire, redefining how the world operates, and reshaping daily interactions.

The second and third blessings continue in the same shocking manner. God is rearranging all the furniture. The blessed poor are elaborated now as the hungry (not fussy foodies) and those who weep (not those who laugh). To be poor is often to be hungry since access to food commonly follows lines of power. The successful have abundance while the poor struggle on a daily basis for sustenance. God-at-work somehow blesses the hungry.

God's favor also embraces those who weep. Who are these people? To be poor materially, lacking resources and options, impacts people not only somatically but also psychologically. Matthew's beatitude, "blessed are the poor in spirit" recognizes both of these dimensions, literal poverty and the damage it does to the human spirit in despair and hopelessness (Matt 5:3). To weep expresses the experience of despair in the midst of poverty. Psalm 35 emphasizes the impact of social marginalization. The psalmist laments that "my soul is forlorn" as a result of the hostility, mocking, and social rejection he experiences from some "enemies," an experience that causes him to be in "mourning" (Ps 35:11-14).

Both of these beatitudes announce God's blessing, but the reversal from God's intervention is constructed as future. The hungry *will be filled* and those who weep *will laugh*. The first beatitude affirmed that God's kingdom or reign is already present and at work, so the use of the future tense adds a further dimension to God's present activity. The future tense anticipates the completion of God's purposes in creating a world in which all have sufficient nutrition and all are free from the damage and pain of inequities of power.

God's future world is commonly portrayed as an abundant feast. The image constructs God as reversing the situations of the poor, hungry, and weeping by providing a very different world for all people:

> On this mountain the LORD of hosts will make for all peoples a feast of rich food, a feast of well-aged wines, of rich food filled with marrow, of well-aged wines strained clear. And he will destroy on this mountain the shroud that is cast over all peoples, the sheet that is spread over all nations; he will swallow up death forever. Then the Lord GOD will wipe away the tears from all faces, and the disgrace of his people he will take away from all the earth, for the LORD has spoken. It will be said on that day, Lo, this is our God; we have waited for him, so that he might save us. This is the LORD for whom we have waited; let us be glad and rejoice in his salvation. (Isa 25:6-9)

These three beatitudes construct God's favor among those who were often socially rejected and disadvantaged. The fourth beatitude recognizes this situation in which unidentified people "hate you, and when they exclude you, revile you, and defame you" (Luke 6:22). God's blessing embraces this situation; their social rejection is not an expression of God's rejection. Rather the situation of social rejection reflects that the powerful and wealthy have rejected God's purposes, just as the prophets had been rejected previously. And as we have seen, God promises a reward in reversing this situation.

Luke 6:24-26: Four Woes

After four declarations of God's blessings that reverse the status quo in favor of the poor and powerless, four woes follow. Woes declare not God's blessing but coming disasters that express God-at-work in bringing about rebuke or judgment. This is the flip side of the reversal work God performs through blessing as God reshapes a new world.

The woes create pairings with the beatitudes. While God blesses the poor, God brings woe or reversal of fortune on the rich. Such a claim continues the startling reversals of the blessings. The biblical tradition often declares wealth and abundance to be God's blessing:

> The LORD will make you abound in prosperity, in the fruit of your womb, in the fruit of your livestock, and the fruit of your ground in the land that the LORD swore to your ancestors to give you. (Deut 28:11-12)

Who are the rich? Mary's song parallels the rich with the powerful and contrasts them with the lowly or powerless and hungry (Luke 1:52-53). In the parable of the "rich fool" that Jesus tells, the rich man has many resources and possessions: land, barns, crops (Luke 12:13-21). In instructions about hospitality, Jesus equates friends with rich neighbors and contrasts them with "the poor, the crippled, the lame, and the blind" (Luke 14:12-13). In another parable, the rich man displays his wealth and status in fine clothes, fine food, "good things," and arrogant disregard for the suffering of the poor. So the rich designates both an economic category marked by and displayed in significant levels of wealth as well as an elite societal location comprising social power and privilege.

This privileged way of life constitutes their consolation or comfort. But God-at-work is reversing this situation, turning their fullness into hunger, their celebration into weeping, their fine reputations and popular acclaim into no account.

These beatitudes and woes provide striking examples of God-at-work. They offer alternatives to the conventional structures of the world. They imagine God-at-work constructing a world without poverty and where justice marks human interactions. Is this how it is?

Questions for Reflection/Discussion

1. Where in our world might we see God-at-work in the ways celebrated in this song (privileging the poor, powerless, and oppressed and shaping a new world marked by equality)? Does God really intervene in national and international affairs? Does God act on behalf of the poor and empower them for better lives while countering the rich and privileged? If so why are there still so many poor folks? How do those who are rich and privileged respond to that bias? Does God act against the powerful and rich to punish them or to rehabilitate them for a world community marked by justice and equality? Does God act on God's own or does God partner with human agents and agencies in doing this work for justice?

2. How do people employ biblical imagery and language to present their own actions as those of God-at-work?

3. How does the construction of God-at-work in these two passages compare with other biblical passages that present reversals of human structures either by God's actions (1 Sam 2:1-10; Ps 107:28-43) or by human actions (Isa 58:1-12)?

4. What constructions of God-at-work are evident in other passages in Luke's Gospel that take up the "reversal of fortune" theme: social relationships (Luke 14:7-24), the interaction of the rich and poor (16:19-31), social status (18:9-14), and the exaltation of the crucified Jesus (Luke 22–24)?

5. Two of the beatitudes (nos. 2 and 3; Luke 6:21-22) and two of the woes (nos. 2 and 3; 6:25) employ future tenses, anticipating

God and the Powerful and the Powerless (Luke 1:47-58; 6:20-26)

God's reversal of these situations in some future time when God's purposes are established in full. This eschatological way of thinking can be understood as "pie in the sky when you die"—encouraging people to ignore present sufferings, to be passive about evil in our world, and to simply await God's future intervention. Do Luke's beatitudes and woes counter this understanding in any way?

Further Reading

Warren Carter and Amy-Jill Levine, "Luke," in *The New Testament: Methods and Meanings* (Nashville: Abingdon, 2013), 54–71.

Chapter 7

Praying to What Sort of God? (Luke 11:1-13; Matt 6:5-15)

> *Read Luke 11:1-13 before reading this chapter. Then refer to it while you read the chapter.*

Encountering God—or struggling to encounter God—in prayer is fundamental to the Judeo-Christian and Islamic traditions. Various forms of prayer approach God in different ways—with praise, confession of sin, petition and request, and lament and disappointment. One morning prayer of petition goes like this:

> Dear Lord, so far this morning I am doing well. I have not been nasty nor lost my temper nor gossiped about anyone nor been greedy, grumpy, selfish, or mean. I have not oppressed anyone. However, I am going to get out of bed in a few minutes, and then I will need a lot more help. Amen.

To talk about prayer is to talk about God. What sort of God is encountered in prayer? For some, prayer is a necessary but unfathomable mystery in which the ways of God remain inscrutable. For others, prayer accesses a God who seems to happily grant whatever they ask: "help me" prayers get answered, parking spaces materialize, healings happen, job offers flow. For others, it seems prayer brings no response from a distant and disinterested God: exams don't go any better; disasters keep happening;

relationships don't flourish. God seems unconcerned about daily dilemmas. Others desperately want to know the key to prayer so that God will do whatever they want. To think about prayer is to think about how we understand God-at-work.

This is also the case in Luke 11. When Jesus's disciples ask him to "teach us to pray," Jesus responds with teaching about God. Yes, he provides them with a prayer to say, but that prayer (11:2-4) and the instructions that follow (11:5-13) construct a particular understanding of God. Jesus does not say, "Don't bother praying because God does not listen to people" or "Don't bother praying because God is so mysterious the whole thing is a lottery." Rather, in instructing his followers to pray, Jesus constructs a God who is relentlessly generous, a loving Father who eagerly gives good gifts to people.

Contexts

We have two forms of the Lord's Prayer in the New Testament, one in Matthew 6 and one here in Luke 11. Not only do the two forms have different content (seven petitions in Matthew; five in Luke), but they also have different contexts. Here in Luke, the lead-in is very brief. Jesus has been praying (Luke 11:1) as he does regularly throughout the Gospel (5:16; 6:12; 9:18, 28), and a disciple asks Jesus for instruction about prayer. Jesus responds with this model prayer. The prayer is introduced as imitating Jesus's habit of prayer.

In Matthew, the lead-in is much longer and more polemical. As part of the Sermon on the Mount, Jesus begins his instruction on prayer with two negative scenarios introduced by "do not." The first scenario contrasts the way hypocrites pray with genuine prayer: "Do not be like the hypocrites" (Matt 6:5-6). Jesus condemns hypocrites whom he constructs as praying in order to impress others with their spirituality rather than seeking genuine encounters with God.

The second scenario mocks Gentiles whose style of praying is said to "heap up empty phrases" (Matt 6:7-8). Do not do "as the Gentiles do." Of course, not all Gentiles prayed with empty phrases, so the description is exaggerated and somewhat unkind. Just what these "empty phrases" might be is not entirely clear. Perhaps "empty phrases" refers to the practice of addressing multiple gods. Or perhaps some who prayed used sequences of syllables or "magic phrases" that they thought constituted the language of the gods. Or perhaps they thought that with long prayers of many words they would get the gods' attention and favor. Whatever they were doing, Jesus points to an alternative practice of prayer grounded in trusting a God who sees, knows, and responds to human needs.

The Lord's Prayer

Jesus's prayer addresses God as Father. Matthew's version includes the pronoun "Our Father" to heighten the communal rather than individual nature of the prayer. Luke's version leaves out this possessive pronoun, suggesting the prayer and the God it addresses are not the property of any particular community. Matthew also includes the traditional qualifying phrase "who is in heaven" that signifies God's otherness apart from and beyond earthly human beings.

Identifying God as Father has had a mixed and controversial history for various reasons.[1] It is a very old and multilayered metaphor for God. It is used as an address for God in other prayers, often along with other forms of address as in this example:

> King of great power, Almighty God Most High, governing all creation with mercy, look upon the descendants of Abraham, O Father (3 Macc 6:2-3; also Sir 23:1, 4).

The image of father names God as Israel's progenitor or founder in bringing Israel into being, as well as into covenant relationship with God: "Is not he [God] your father, who created you, who made you and established you?" (Deut 32:6). Establishing a covenant relationship suggests adoption by and relationship with God, who as father heads a household of God's children (Deut 14:1). Such a relationship embodies (in part) a dynamic of authority and obedience whereby God imparts God's rules, which people are to obey. Obedience is rewarded with blessing; disobedience brings punishment (Deut 28).

But this relationship is also marked by God's love for God's children, even when the children are rebellious (Hos 11:1). In a mixed gender move, Hosea presents God the Father acting like a loving and nurturing mother toward Israel as a disobedient child, even vowing to "not execute my fierce anger":

> I took them up in my arms; but they did not know that I healed them. I led them with cords of human kindness, with bands of love. I was to them like those who lift infants to their cheeks. I bent down to them and fed them. ... [M]y compassion grows warm and tender. (Hos 11:3-4, 8)

Punishment or discipline in this father-child relationship is seen as a means of correction and expression of God's love for those in whom God the Father "delights" (Prov 3:12). God's compassion means that God recognizes human finitude and weakness:

> As a father has compassion for his children, so the LORD has compassion for those who fear him. For he knows how we were made; he remembers that we are dust. (Psa 103:13-14)

This construction of God as Father, to whom the prayer is addressed, is, then, a multidimensional metaphor.

The issue of what language we should use for God has been a contentious one. This father-child relationship is not the only way of representing our human interaction with God. An alternative model, for example, sees humans as partners with God-at-work in the world (Phil 2:12-13). But the metaphor "father" has been a common and pervasive metaphor, and often a painful and **Red-flag issue** for women. Those who have had bad relationships or experiences with their (abusive) human fathers are distressed by this cosmic-sized Father God. One troubling dimension involves the great authority that this Father God wields in these biblical texts, rendering humans as subservient children who will be punished if they displease "daddy." And presenting that painful punishment as a display of love rarely persuades anyone.

Another troubling dimension centers on the gendering of God as male that inscribes a system of and sanction for patriarchal dominance over women. The metaphor "father" can turn God into an authoritarian male to whom people, including women, must submit. Often this image bears patriarchal weight in being the only or dominant image used by churches for God. Such use excludes feminine images for God. This monopoly has the effect for some women of excluding them from ecclesial communities.

In a nuanced discussion, Gail O'Day recognizes these troubling issues in the use of male images and pronouns for God.[2] She especially laments the exclusive use of father language because it not only ignores numerous other images for God but also loses the particularity of this image and its appropriateness for some situations. She notes that father language can be, but need not always be, patriarchal in reinscribing male dominance. She points out that it can also be language of relationship, of intimacy, of compassion, and of a family or household that welcomes and includes outsiders. The context in which it is used in biblical texts will often provide some clue as to its meaning.

The Rest of the Prayer

The rest of the prayer expands the construction of God. The first petition is introduced with a strange verb, "hallowed be your name." The petition recognizes that God's name and God's being are the same. The verb "hallow" has to do with sanctifying or setting someone or something apart for divine service. Here the verb asks God to sanctify Godself, to act faithfully in carrying out God's purposes. That is, the petition recognizes that in current circumstances God is not honored, but it also urges God to be more proactive, to be busy in carrying out God's purposes. It petitions God to get busy, to be God-at-work in the world.

The second petition, "your kingdom come," similarly constructs God in terms of God's activity. The image of father now gives way to the image of God as a ruling king or emperor. The petition asks God to assert God's rule over all that is contrary to God's will for creation, the sorts of situations and structures we identified in the discussion in the last chapter of Mary's song (Luke 1:47-55) and the beatitudes and woes (Luke 6:20-26). In the context of the Roman world in which the Roman Empire or kingdom dominated, this is a subversive petition.

How is the petition to be answered? Jesus has been announcing God's kingdom or reign in his activity since Luke 4:43. He has been repairing the damage of imperial practices in his healings, exorcisms, feedings, and teachings. He has been forming an alternative and inclusive community. These actions suggest that God's assertion of God's reign does not belong to God exclusively, but it happens in partnership with God's agents like Jesus and the community of his disciples whom Jesus commissions to continue his activity (Luke 9:1-2).

Matthew's version of the prayer adds another petition at this point: "Your will be done on earth as it is in heaven" (Matt 6:10). The petition reinforces the sense of God the king establishing God's reign on earth. Heaven is imagined as a place where God's reign and will are already established. The petition in Matthew's prayer asks God to extend them to earth among human beings.

Luke's version of the prayer now offers three petitions concerning human needs (Luke 11:3-4). The first of these petitions again changes the image of God, from father to king to provider or sustainer of life. The petition asks God to provide "daily bread" or "bread for the coming day." The need for the petition arises out of the situation in which many did not have basic necessities on a daily basis. The Roman imperial world was hierarchical in structure, meaning ruling elites controlled the production and distribution of food through land ownership, slaves, taxes/tariffs, and access to markets.[3] This system meant that elites ate well while poor folks struggled to varying degrees to secure adequate daily nutrition. Lack of nutrition meant susceptibility to diseases of deprivation and contagion.

The petition again constructs God as one who challenges imperial ways. One of the ways in which the petition is answered involves restructured human communities. It is a petition against the powerful who hoard resources and consider themselves entitled to a superior and secure way of life without regard for the needs of others. It urges people to create communities in which mutual responsibility and sharing of resources, however meager, are normative practices. God answers in a world restructured to ensure compassion and justice.

Praying to What Sort of God? (Luke 11:1-13; Matt 6:5-15)

The second of the three petitions asks God to forgive sins. The verb *forgive* has meanings such as "send away," "cancel," "let go"; its cognate noun "forgiveness" means "release." God is constructed as the one who sends away sins, who releases people from the identity and obligations of their sinfulness, who does not hold this offense against people: "As far as the east is from the west so far he removes our transgressions from us" (Ps 103:12). Interestingly, the receiving of the gift of God's forgiveness manifests itself in the forgiveness that humans extend to each other.

The third of the three petitions asks God to "not bring us to the time of trial." Just what God is being asked to do is complicated by the difficulty of how to translate the last phrase. The word could be translated "temptation" so that the petition asks God not to lead us into temptation. But what sort of God leads people into temptation with the risk of sinning? That does not make much sense. Other New Testament texts rightly reject the idea that God tempts people (Jas 1:13-14).

Another possible translation is that of "trial" or "test." A long tradition exists across the Bible that God tests believers and followers to strengthen their trust in and relationship with God. So God tests Abraham's obedience and trust in the very troubling scene of offering his son Isaac as a sacrifice (Gen 22). In another very troubling scenario, God tests Job's loyalty by letting the figure called the satan take away Job's property, children, and health (Job 1–2). Such a construction of God who plays with people's lives in such cruel ways is hardly an attractive or compelling image of God. This God does not seem trustworthy. This is a **Red-flag moment**.

A third and more convincing option suggests another scenario for this "time of trial." This scenario concerns God's apparent lack of activity in transforming the world, which causes people to doubt and despair. An incident occurs in Exodus 17 where the people at a place called Massah in the wilderness find no water and doubt God's intentions to care for them. The lack of water suggests God's apparent inactivity or God's absence or God's powerlessness. This apparent passivity causes the people to doubt and despair that God can make any difference. In this light, this final petition prays for God's transforming activity to be active and evident in the world when the world's injustice and evil suggests God's inactivity or powerlessness or lack of intervention. It prays that God be actively hallowing God's name, establishing God's reign, feeding people, and forgiving sin. If God's will is to establish God's reign and purposes, why has God not done so yet? Is the world's evil too powerful or overwhelming for God? Has God lost the plot? Is God low on power? Does God have burnout and not care anymore? The petition seeks God's relentless and gracious activity to counter such disillusionment and hopelessness so that the untransformed world does not bring believers to a time of trial in despairing of God's purposes and power.[4]

The prayer has constructed God as a father, as king or ruler, as provider of life-sustaining nutrition in the midst of and as a challenge to imperial structures, as the one who forgives sin, and as the one whose active intervention is desperately needed.

Persistent Praying or Generous God?

Two scenes follow that continue the construction of God as a generous, loving father who eagerly and generously gives good gifts to people.

The first scenario or parable invites readers to imagine a scene in which an unexpected guest arrives at your house at night but you have no food to offer your guest (Luke 11:5-8). This is an embarrassing and shameful situation. So you ask your neighbor for help so that you don't lose face or standing in the eyes of your guest and community. But your neighbor refuses to help, claiming to have already gone to bed with the kids (Luke 11:5-7). The neighbor-friend's refusal to help is utterly improbable given village norms for hospitality, expectations of material assistance in friendship, and the strong sense of honor that prevents shameful behaviors in social interactions. By not helping, the friend-neighbor loses face and social standing. Verse 8 makes the point by reversing and correcting the situation. "Because he is his friend," he will not behave shamefully, stay in bed, and let himself be shamed as a bad neighbor and let his friend be dishonored as a bad host. "He will get up and give [his friend] whatever he needs" (11:8).

In the NRSV translation, this verse makes a strange reference to the role of "his persistence."[5] Whose "persistence" is in view is not clear, but perhaps that of the host in pursuing the neighbor in bed might be the better option. However, there are two problems. The short scene did not show any of the characters exhibiting persistence. And second, the word probably does not mean "persistence" anyway. More likely it means "shamelessness." But who is shameless—the host in asking for help or the neighbor in initially refusing help? The better option is probably the latter one. The guy-in-bed realizes that his refusal to help is shameful and recognizes that the honorable thing to do is to get up and provide the bread his neighbor-friend needs.

The parable invites readers to compare the neighbor with God. If the neighbor will do the honorable thing and help his friend with what he needs, how much more will God readily and generously assist those who pray. God is trustworthy, generous, and loving in providing good gifts in response to prayer. The issue is not human persistence but the character of God.

Luke 11:9-10 elaborates this confidence in God, who responds graciously to prayer with good gifts. Three repeated pairings state the principle: people ask, search, and knock; God gives, is found, and opens.

Another scenario illustrates the principle. The scenario again uses a household scene, again employs an improbable situation, and again draws a contrast with God's character and actions (Luke 11:11-13). The verse appeals to commonsense human behavior. If a child asks a parent for food such as fish or an egg, no parent will respond by giving a very unhealthy snack like a snake or scorpion. Luke 11:13 draws out the point by arguing from the lesser situation to the greater. If human parents with all our imperfections know "to give good gifts to your children, how much more" does God the generous and loving heavenly Father know how to do so (11:13). God's goodness and giving of good gifts far exceeds that of human abilities. And God's superiority stretches even to the quality of the good gifts. God gives the Holy Spirit. Just how this gift is made is not elaborated here but it will be subsequently in Acts 1–2.

The emphasis in this passage has been on God-at-work as gracious, relentless, and generous in giving the best "good gifts" to those who approach God in prayer. We might draw the conclusion that we have now figured out the mystery of prayer and solved the "how-to-get-what-we-want-in-prayer" conundrum. Luke 11:9-10, 13 suggests God is simply bubbling over with the desire to dispense the best "good gifts" in response to anyone who asks in prayer!

However—the **Red flag** is waving—two factors urge caution and require us to reintroduce the notion of mystery. First, our human experience of prayer tells us it is not so simple. Many have prayed earnestly and with faith for noble outcomes and divine interventions only to find their prayer is not answered the way they wanted it to be. And second, Luke 11:8 perhaps qualifies this divine bubbliness. The friend gives the host "whatever he needs"—three loaves of bread—not any and everything. He doesn't, for example, hand over his house and land. So here's the rub—God's generous bubbliness embraces what humans "need." Does God alone decide what humans need? Does a generous God ever go beyond human need to provide "what we want" or "what we think we deserve"?

Questions for Reflection/Discussion

1. Take up the issue in the last paragraph. How might these factors—God's generous and willing response to prayer, the determination of human need, and the place of human desire and deserving—interact in a construction of God in this passage?

2. This passage emphasizes God-at-work in generous and gracious manner in giving the best "good gifts." A parable in Luke 18:1-8 presents another perspective that emphasizes not God's character but human persistence. Do these presentations sit together?

3. The biblical tradition includes numerous prayers that construct God in various ways. Read Tobit 13 in the Apocrypha. Verse 4 identifies God as Father. What other constructions emerge in the prayer? Why are some images more popular than others?

Praying to What Sort of God? (Luke 11:1-13; Matt 6:5-15)

Further Reading

John Carroll, "The God of Israel and the Salvation of the Nations: The Gospel of Luke and the Acts of the Apostles," in *The Forgotten God: Perspectives in Biblical Theology*, ed. Andrew Das and Frank Matera (Louisville: Westminster John Knox, 2002), 91–106.

Richard N. Longenecker, ed., *Into God's Presence: Prayer in the New Testament* (Grand Rapids: Eerdmans, 2001).

Chapter 8

How to Dishonor God (John 5:1-30)

> *Read John 5:1-30 before reading this chapter.
> Reference it while you read the chapter.*

Paul Simon sang that there are "fifty ways to leave your lover." Websites list "twenty-five ways to say 'I love you'" or "twelve ways to lose weight" or "seven steps to happiness."

How many ways are there to dishonor God? What sort of God gets dishonored? What's at stake in dishonoring God? Why does it matter? For whom does it matter? These questions emerge in John chapter 5 from Jesus's initial healing action (5:1-15) and his subsequent debate with the Jerusalem-based leaders (5:16-30).

The scene opens with Jesus in Jerusalem. We have learned much about Jesus in the previous four chapters of John's Gospel. The central claim appears at the end of the Gospel's crucial opening prologue: "No one has ever seen God. It is God the only Son, who is close to the Father's heart who has made him known" (1:18).

The premise of the verse is that people find God unknown and invisible. God needs someone to make God known to people. In order to make a reliable and trustworthy revelation of God, this revealer needs the best qualifications. The verse asserts the choice of Jesus, the Son or agent of God, as God's revealer. And it elaborates his credentials to be a trustworthy revealer of God, namely his intimate knowledge of God gained from being "close to the Father's heart." This intimate relationship is reflected in John's Gospel, presenting Jesus and God as being "one" (10:30), as being "in" each other (14:10-11) in a relationship of love (3:35) whereby to know or see one is to know or see the other (14:7, 9). Yet as this passage will emphasize in 5:19-30, Jesus is also subordinate to God. The perspective that God is revealed in the words and actions of Jesus frames the whole of John's Gospel, including this scene in chapter 5 where the claim is both asserted and contested.

Jesus comes to Jerusalem as the revealer of God. But there is already a revelation of God in Jerusalem. It is centered on the temple and its leaders comprising the chief priests, priests, and Levites. The offerings and sacrifices of daily worship and annual festivals such as Passover (John 2:13), Tabernacles/Booths (John 7:2), and Dedication (John 10:22) revealed God and provided encounter with God. Israel's sacred writings narrated God-at-work in these events. Passover celebrated the revelation of God in delivering the people from slavery in Egypt. Tabernacles or Booths celebrated the revelation of God's presence with the people and gracious provision of food for them in the wilderness. Dedication or Hanukkah celebrated the revelation of God's power in liberating Jerusalem from the Syrian tyrant Antiochus IV Epiphanes. Antiochus had defiled the temple and with Jerusalem's liberation its temple was rededicated (1 Macc 4:36-59).

How do these various revelations in Jerusalem—those centered in the temple and those centered in Jesus—interact?

John's Gospel is not very respectful of the revelation in the temple. The Gospel presents the temple personnel as being vigilant but in the task of spying on other public figures (John 1:19-28)! And Jesus challenges the way they administer the temple, attacking them for making it into a "marketplace," claiming it as "my Father's house" (2:13-22), and declaring he will destroy it (2:19). This is not the way to win friends! So in entering Jerusalem in John 5:1, Jesus returns to the city in which he has already conflicted with these powerful political-religious leaders of Judea. What will happen?

How to Dishonor God (John 5:1-30)

God: Giver of Life or Punisher of Sin?

Another question concerning the revelation of God emerges in John 5:2-3. In Jerusalem, Jesus goes to a pool called Bethsaida in whose porticoes lie "many invalids—blind, lame, and paralyzed." For some unspecified reason, Jesus focuses on one man "who had been ill for thirty-eight years" and had not been able to enter the pool for healing. It's his lucky day! Jesus heals him, telling him to take up his mat and walk—which the man does successfully. Since Jesus is the revealer of God, the healing displays God-at-work. Jesus reveals God as the giver of new life to this man—physically, socially, and economically.

Jesus, though, makes a disturbing comment to the healed man: "See, you have been made well! Do not sin anymore, so that nothing worse happens to you" (John 5:14). What is Jesus saying? His instruction to the man not to "sin anymore" and his threat of possible worse consequences if he does indicate that Jesus explains the man's thirty-eight years of paralysis as resulting from his sin.

The **Red flag** is waving. This claim reveals a very disturbing way in which God was understood to be at-work. God punished sinful people by afflicting them with disabilities and illness!

> But if you will not obey the LORD your God by diligently observing all his commandments and decrees . . . the LORD will send upon you disaster, panic and frustration . . . on account of the evil of your deeds. . . . The LORD will make a pestilence cling to you . . . The LORD will afflict you with consumption, fever, inflammation . . . with boils . . . ulcers, scurvy and itch of which you cannot be treated . . . with madness, blindness and confusion of mind . . . The LORD will strike you on the knees and on the legs with grievous boils from which you cannot be healed, from the sole of your foot to the crown of your head. You will be untreatable. (Deut 28:15-35 selections)

To be fair, four chapters later, Jesus denies that a man's blindness was caused by the man's or his parents' sin (9:3a). But here in chapter 5, he clearly says that the man's disability results from divine punishment for his sin. This claim is like the toothpaste. Once it's out of the tube there's no putting it back in! This claim that disability and human suffering result from divine punishment for sin constructs a terrible, vindictive, punitive, and scary God. Of course, this image is at odds with the God who heals and gives new life to this man. It dishonors a God who heals disabled bodies and imparts new life.

Sabbath and God's Honor

John 5:9 introduces a key piece of information and a further dimension to the issue of dishonoring God. The narrator informs us that the healing happened on the Sabbath. Sabbath, the seventh day, was understood to be instituted by God as a day of rest from work in order to honor God. Sabbath was not just a religious matter; it was a fundamental structure of Jewish life and society.

This work-free Sabbath was justified in two ways. First, it imitated God's practice of creating for six days and resting on the seventh (Gen 2:1-3). In one of the ten commandments that God gave to Moses, God ordered: "You shall not do any work—you, your son or daughter, your male or female slave, your livestock, or the alien resident [it could be translated "immigrant"] in your towns" (Exod 20:8-10). The Sabbath day also became a Sabbath year every seven years and a Jubilee year every fifty years (seven times seven years). These years, if they were activated, were to enact significant socioeconomic practices of freeing slaves, cancelling debts, and redistributing land (Exod 21:2-6; 23:10-11; Lev 25).

Second, the Sabbath day honored God as the one who liberated the Israelites from slavery in Egypt:

> But the seventh day is a Sabbath to the LORD your God; you shall not do any work . . . Remember that you were a slave in the land of Egypt, and the LORD your God brought you out from there with a mighty hand and an outstretched arm; therefore the LORD your God commanded you to keep the Sabbath day. (Deut 5:14-15)

This second rationale honored God as Israel's savior or redeemer in rescuing the people from slavery in Egypt.

The observance of the Sabbath was a distinctive marker of Jewish identity. It marked Israel as a people in covenant relationship with God, a favored people, distinct and separate from Gentiles (Exod 31:16). It celebrated God-at-work in the world as creator and as Israel's savior from oppressive nations. It provided meaning for and orchestrated the rhythm of weekly life. Some Gentiles mocked it as a weird practice fostering laziness, but for Jewish folks, it had great importance.

But it was not without its challenges. What did it mean not to work? What daily practices were forbidden, and which ones, if any, were permitted? Did everyone know? Who made these decisions? Who benefitted, and who got hurt by them? Were poor folks who struggled to earn a living day-by-day disadvantaged by the requirement of rest? Did they observe it? Were others protected from overwork? In what other circumstances might Sabbath not be observed?[1]

Monitoring the Sabbath asserted the power of the Jerusalem-based leadership. In this passage, the man, after he has been healed, picks up and carries his mat as he walks. The authorities, called "the Jews," tell the man this is not lawful behavior (John 5:8-15).

We have to be very careful—**Red-flag alert**—with this term translated as "the Jews." It's easy for non-Jewish, especially Christian, readers to understand the designation in ethnic terms, but that is not how the Gospel uses it. Jesus is a Jew and the healed man is a Jew, but neither of them belongs to this group. So Jewishness or ethnicity is not the issue. The term "the Jews" in the Gospel is not an ethnic term.[2]

In the previous chapters, it refers to the power group, the rulers of Judea, based in Jerusalem and the temple (John 1:19; 2:20; 3:1). They are sociopolitical and religious leaders, the Judean elite. They present themselves as God's sanctioned representatives with responsibility for how their society is structured.

Because of their sociopolitical and religious position as Judean leaders, they have vested interests in Sabbath observance. They care greatly about and monitor its observance. So they inform the healed man that he has broken the law by carrying a load, and they learn from him that he has been misled to do so by an unauthorized teacher/healer named Jesus (John 5:10-15). Immediately they want to kill Jesus (5:16-18). He has threatened their authority and their vision of how the Sabbath should be observed. As far as they are concerned, he has no authority to offer false teaching about the Sabbath that so clearly misrepresents—and dishonors—God.

In this conflict, it is easy for Christian readers automatically to side with Jesus and to see "the Jews" in negative terms. But it's important to take them seriously in order to understand the issue. Both sides value Sabbath observance. Both sides want to honor God in Sabbath observance and to avoid dishonoring God. God matters to both sides very much.

"The Jews" present themselves as the rightful custodians of the tradition, its true interpreters, committed to Sabbath as a day of rest that imitates God's practice of resting after six days of creation. Imitating God is a powerful justification for their insistence that God be honored with a day of rest. What's good enough for God is surely good enough for people. It's also a powerful motivation for their wanting to shut Jesus down as one who offers teaching and practices that dishonor the Sabbath and God in their view (John 5:16).

Jesus offers a different perspective on how God is to be honored on the Sabbath. His perspective and practice are rooted in a different understanding of God. Instead of framing Sabbath observance in terms of rest, he frames it in terms of the life-giving God continuing to be at-work. He recasts God as actively and compassionately present in the world, even on the Sabbath.

He declares, "My Father is still working, and I also am working" (John 5:17). The claim that even God worked on the Sabbath and did not just rest was not a new thought. Folks understood that births and deaths on the Sabbath were God's actions of giving and taking away life. But Jesus puts the notion of God's continuing activity center stage. And in healing the paralyzed man, he emphasizes that God-at-work, when that happens, is not only life-giving but also compassionate. That is, Jesus frames the Sabbath as not just remembering God's creative activity in the past but also the occasion for God's continuing life-giving, creative, and compassionate work in the present.

This redefinition of God challenges their authority. But Jesus makes a further claim that escalates the conflict: "and I also am working" (John 5:17b). With this claim, Jesus asserts his ongoing participation in and continuing partnership with God-at-work as the revealer of God's life-giving and compassionate activity. He counters the accusation that he was *breaking* the law about the Sabbath and dishonoring God. As far as Jesus is concerned, he is *interpreting* the law and honoring both the Sabbath and God.

Before moving on, we should recall that God's work embraces only one person in the crowd at the pool. What about the rest? Jesus ignores them. God's power and compassion doesn't seem to extend to them. That's a concern. The **Red flag** is waving.

Jesus's claim that he is working like God infuriates the authorities. Instead of hearing an invitation to rethink their understanding of God-at-rest, they see Jesus dishonoring the Sabbath, God, and themselves as societal leaders. They accuse him of calling God *his own* Father and making himself equal with God (John 5:18). So what's their problem?

As we have seen in the previous chapter, calling God "Father" was common. The force of their objection is expressed in the words *his own*. They think Jesus claims a special relationship with God that goes beyond the usual. So they charge him with "making himself equal to God." In their eyes, this most serious charge dishonors God terribly because it suggests that there are two gods (bitheism).

Basic to Jewish understanding of God is the notion of monotheism, that there is *one* God. This confession is expressed in the *Shema*: "Hear, O Israel: The LORD is our God, the LORD alone. You shall love the LORD your God with all your heart, and with all your soul, and with all your might" (Deut 6:4-5). To suggest that there are two or more gods, or to acknowledge "other" gods, is a shocking way to dishonor Israel's God. This confession of one God was, like Sabbath observance, a marker of Israel's distinctive identity among the nations where polytheism was the norm.

Excuse Me, Your Piety Is Showing

In their eyes, Jesus's violation of the Sabbath, dishonoring of God, and threat to their societal vision merits killing him (John 5:18). Why such a drastic response? Are they lashing out against Jesus in blind rage?

The explanation lies elsewhere—in their spirituality or piety. Their piety centered on honoring God. That means protecting God's honor or reputation against those they understand to dishonor God—even if that meant killing them. The scriptures informed this piety of honorable killing. It required the death of anyone who appeared to dishonor God—especially by recognizing or worshipping other gods and violating the Sabbath. In their view Jesus is such a person.

A number of biblical passages sustain this piety of killing those who dishonor God by advocating worship of other gods. A prophet who advocates this practice "shall be put to death for having spoken treason against the LORD your God" (Deut 13:1-5). Anyone, even someone in your own family, who encourages worshipping other gods, is to be put to death (Deut 13:6-11).

Likewise a number of biblical passages sustain a piety of killing those who dishonor God by not resting on the Sabbath:

> Six days shall work be done but the seventh day is a Sabbath of solemn rest, holy to the LORD; whoever does any work on the Sabbath day shall be put to death. (Exod 31:15; also Exod 35:2; Num 15:32-36)

Three episodes show this piety in action. Moses orders the sons of Aaron to kill some three thousand people for false worship (Exod 32, esp. 32:25-29). Moses orders those who worship the god Baal to be killed, and Phinehas drives his spear through an Israelite man and Midianite woman (Num 25). With "righteous anger," Mattathias kills an officer of King Antiochus for urging worship of another god and kills an Israelite man in the act of doing so (1 Macc 2:23-26).

In John 5, they understand Jesus to be guilty of both offenses. He has made himself equal to God, thereby making himself another god. And he has violated the Sabbath with his instruction to the man. Two times he has dishonored God; he deserves to die.

Of course—**Red-flag alert**—violence in the name of God was not just an ancient phenomenon. In our world, troops go to war in the name of various gods. In the United States, providers of abortion services have been killed by those who consider them to dishonor God and who think their death honors God. People have been killed because of their sexual orientation by those who consider it an offense to God.[3] And terrorists have killed many whom they deem to dishonor their God, provoking deathly retaliations. Honoring God, without tolerance for different understandings and practices, is deadly.

John 5:19-30: Jesus Defends Himself

Jesus responds by denying he has made himself equal to God or violated Sabbath. Far from dishonoring God, he argues he honors God by recognizing God legitimates him as God's Son or agent. To make this claim, he appeals to two images of God—as Father and as the one who sent him. Both images construct God-at-work and Jesus as God's Son who honors his Father God as good sons should by being subordinate and obedient.

Jesus claims his revelation of God comprises his being the imitator of God in bestowing life (as he has done to the paralyzed man) and in exercising judgment. He performs these functions because the Father who loves him has tutored him in God's ways (John 5:19-22). And this Father is the dispatcher, the one "who sent him" to reveal God's purposes. This Father God who sends Jesus legitimates and authorizes Jesus's identity, mission, and activity.

These purposes center on revealing "eternal life" or, more literally, "life of the age" (John 5:24). This phrase expresses a distinctive understanding of God-at-work. This understanding divides human existence into two ages, the present age in which the world is not as God intends it, and a new age in which God establishes God's purposes under God's rule. These purposes include the end of sin and death, the end of disease and strife among nations and people, the establishment of good health and abundant fertility, justice and peace, and God's presence among people.

Jesus claims that in his actions he reveals God working for these purposes. The healing of the paralyzed man is not just a display of power and compassion; it reveals God's new age already present in part among people. Far from dishonoring God, Jesus's action honors the Father who sent Jesus by enacting and participating in God's purpose. Jesus declares that commitment to him as God's revealer and agent (Son)—believing—means people participate in God's new age of life now in the present (John 5:24).

In John 5:25-29, Jesus goes on to say more about God-at-work. While this new age is present and accessible by commitment to or believing in God's agent Jesus, God has not yet finished God's work in full. Does this mean God's failure to accomplish God's purposes? Is God too weak or faithless in the face of daily sin and death, disease and strife? Jesus's claim in these verses is that God has simply not yet finished working, that it is important to understand the contours of the schedule. God continues to create this new world and "the hour is coming" when it will be completed. Jesus honors God with confidence in God's power, faithfulness, and compassion to accomplish these purposes.

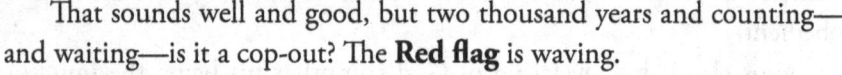

That sounds well and good, but two thousand years and counting—and waiting—is it a cop-out? The **Red flag** is waving.

Questions for Reflection/Discussion

1. There is no doubt that violence in the name of God is a major problem in our world as people claim to avenge God's honor. Review the passages cited in this chapter to identify aspects of the Judeo-Christian contribution to this problem. Note John 5:29's declaration of condemnation (violent destruction) by God that awaits "those who have done evil." What might be done to counter violence in the name of God? What role does violence in the name of God play in contemporary Christian-Muslim relationships?

2. Constructions of God in this passage range from punitive to loving, from resting creator to life-giving activist, from the Father to the dispatcher. Elaborate each of these constructions. Do you see God-at-work in particular ways in our world?

3. If you see someone working on the Sabbath, should you kill him or her as the scriptures command you to do? Why or why not?

4. In its last section, the passage makes much of God's purposes for, or God-at-work in, the world involving "life of the age," giving life, and exercising judgment/condemnation both in the present and future (John 5:19-30). Check out visions of this "life of the age" in Isaiah 25:6-10a and 35:5-7. Do you find these scenes to

offer a compelling vision of God-at-work? What do you make of the affirmations that God both "gives life" and "condemns"? Is the unlimited future of God's purposes a cover-up for God's lack of power and care?

5. This scene might be read as showing that neither party has the whole truth. The Sabbath is a day of rest; the Sabbath honors God's continued creative and life-giving work. Both "the Jews" and Jesus challenge each other to recognize that neither has a monopoly on understanding God-at-work. Do you agree?

6. Where does God-at-work challenge contemporary churches with new understandings and practices?

Further Reading

Francis Moloney, "Telling God's Story: The Fourth Gospel," in *The Forgotten God: Perspectives in Biblical Theology*, ed. Andrew Das and Frank Matera (Louisville: Westminster John Knox, 2002), 107–22.

Marianne Thompson, *The God of the Gospel of John* (Grand Rapids: Eerdmans, 2001).

Chapter 9

Cornelius, Peter, and an (Im)partial God (Acts 10:1–11:18)

> *Read Acts 10:1–11:18 before reading this chapter. Then refer to it while you read the chapter.*

This scene involving the Jew Peter and the conversion of the Gentile Cornelius is vital to the narrative of Acts. It presents the church embracing Jewish *and* Gentile converts. Central to this presentation is the construction of God, who sanctions this embrace. God shows no partiality to either Jew or Gentile (Acts 10:28b, 34) and welcomes Gentiles as well as Jews (Acts 11:18), and no one can hinder God's inclusive purposes (Acts 11:17).

Where the scene occurs in Acts underscores its importance. An instruction from the risen Jesus in chapter 1 provides the structure for Acts. Before he departs to God, the risen Jesus as God's agent promises his followers that the Holy Spirit will come to them with the result that "you will be my witnesses in Jerusalem, in all Judea and Samaria, and to the ends of the earth" (Acts 1:8). Jesus's command identifies an expanding geographical movement; this expansion provides the basis for the structure of Acts. In chapters 1–7 Jesus's followers bear witness in Jerusalem. In chapter 8 they bear witness in Samaria. In chapters 9–28 they bear witness among the non-Jewish or Gentile population throughout the ancient world, even as far as Rome, the center of the empire. The Acts narrative is organized on the basis of Jesus's command.

By chapter 10, the disciples have obediently witnessed in Judea (chs. 1-7) and Samaria (ch. 8). Chapter 9 dramatically presents the conversion of Saul/Paul on the road to Damascus. God declares Paul is to play a key role in the mission to Gentiles:

> Go, for he is an instrument whom I have chosen to bring my name before Gentiles and kings and before the people of Israel. (Acts 9:15)

Paul will be the central figure in the narrative of the Gentile mission in the second half of Acts. But before narrating Paul's activities, chapters 10–11 make very clear that the inclusion of Gentiles is God's idea. God sanctions the mission and Peter has the first go at it.

All of this is to say that the structure of Acts in terms of this threefold geographical organization is actually a theological structure. The risen Jesus announces in Acts 1:8 God's purposes and plans. The narrative shows the accomplishing of God's plans.

Cornelius, Peter, Cornelius, Peter

The Cornelius-Peter narrative in Acts 10:1–11:18 is very repetitive. A series of short scenes both moves the action forward and recalls what has already happened. The repetition underscores the importance of what God is doing with Peter and Cornelius.

Scene 1 (Acts 10:1-8) introduces Cornelius in the coastal town of Caesarea. He is a centurion, a military man in authority over one hundred soldiers. But more significantly, the scene emphasizes his piety. He is devout, fearing or reverencing God, giving alms or charity to the poor, and praying regularly. Appropriately, while he is praying, an angel or messenger from God appears in a vision. The angel instructs him to send some of his people to fetch Simon Peter, who is in the town of Joppa. Cornelius, being devout, obeys the angel and dispatches two slaves and a soldier to find Peter.

Scene 2 (Acts 10:9-16) takes us to Joppa and to Simon Peter. While Cornelius's representatives approach the town, Peter is praying. He becomes hungry, falls into a trance, and has a vision of his own eat-all-you-can buffet in the form of a large sheet containing all kinds of animals, reptiles, and birds coming down from heaven (from God). A voice (God's) tells him to kill and eat. Peter protests that as a faithful Jewish person he would never eat anything "unclean or profane" (Acts 10:14). Here, Peter reminds God of something God had legislated back in Leviticus 11. That chapter catalogues land animals, sea creatures, and birds and God differentiates between "the unclean and the clean and between the living creature that may be eaten and the living creature that may not be eaten" (Lev 11:47). The observance of these "food purity" laws functioned for many Jews as a marker of Jewish identity and distinctiveness from the rest of the nations, just as did Sabbath observance and the worship of one God.

God's reply to Peter in the vision is most surprising: "What God has made clean, you must not call profane" (Acts 10:15). Three times God makes this declaration that all of God's creation on the buffet is good and nothing is profane. The repetition is necessary; we can imagine Peter struggling to believe what he thinks he is hearing. With these words, God seems to break down a huge boundary that God had previously set in place. God is abolishing a division that for centuries had been important for Jewish people—because they believed it was God's will.

What are we to make of God's words? Is God saying that God's instructions in Leviticus 11 now no longer apply and can be ignored? Is God admitting to a mistake and changing God's mind? Or is the author of Acts offering a new insight about God that moves beyond dualistic thinking to a holistic embrace of the goodness of all creation? However we understand God's words in verse 15, the significance of the message that no living creature is unclean is huge.

Scene 3 (Acts 10:17-23a) begins with Peter still "greatly puzzled" about his vision. Then representatives from Cornelius arrive. The Spirit vouches for them, and they repeat Cornelius's experience of being instructed by an angel to send for Peter. Peter welcomes them with hospitality.

Scene 4 (Acts 10:23b-33) brings Peter to Cornelius in Caesarea. Peter repeats the lesson he learned from the eat-all-you-can buffet vision: God has abolished the division between clean and profane, not only in relation to animals and food, but also in relation to people, especially the division between Jews and Gentiles (10:28). On this basis, Peter readily welcomes the Gentile Cornelius's group.[1] Cornelius responds by repeating for the third time his experience of God instructing him to send for Peter. He declares his group ready, in the presence of God, to hear what Peter has to say.

In scene 5 (Acts 10:34-48), Peter preaches. The sermon provides the theological framework for what is happening in the scene and for the larger mission to Gentiles. Peter declares "that God shows no partiality" or favor for only some people but not for others (10:34). He affirms that God finds acceptable "in every nation anyone who fears him and does what is right" (10:35). Then he summarizes Jesus's activity as the one whom "God anointed" or commissioned: "how he went about doing good and healing all who were oppressed by the devil, for God was with him. We are witnesses to all that he did both in Judea and in Jerusalem. They put him to death by hanging him on a tree, but God raised him on the third day and allowed him to appear . . . to us who were chosen by God as witnesses" (10:38-40).

He also summarizes the disciples' preaching activity in response to the risen Jesus's command.

While Peter is preaching, the Holy Spirit "fell upon all who heard the word." They speak in tongues as evidence for the Spirit's presence (Acts 10:44-46). The Jewish believers are astounded that God has given the Spirit to Gentiles, but the event plays out Peter's declaration that "God shows no partiality." The Gentile believers are baptized in water, a sign of their inclusion into the community of Jesus-followers.

Scene 6 (Acts 11:1-18) repeats the whole scene for the benefit of the (Jewish) apostles and believers in Jerusalem. This group is upset that Peter has baptized "uncircumcised men" and "eaten with them." They have heard that Peter has disregarded markers of Jewish identity, namely circumcision and food purity, and welcomed Gentile believers with baptism without requiring them to become Jews. Peter's welcome changes the identity of the Jesus movement. It is no longer an intra-Jewish group but a cosmopolitan or international group embodying the all-inclusive purposes of a God who shows no partiality to one ethnic group.

By way of explanation, "step-by-step," Peter rehearses for them (and for us as readers) what happened in chapter 10. He starts with his own buffet vision of the sheet coming down from heaven and God's threefold announcement abolishing the division of clean and profane (Acts 11:4-10). He narrates Cornelius's experience of an angel telling him to send for Peter (11:11-14). Then he summarizes his preaching, the Spirit falling on the Gentiles, and Peter baptizing them (11:15-16). He gives his theological justification that the presence of the Spirit indicates God's gracious gift to and acceptance of the Gentiles: "Who was I that I could hinder God?"

The scene ends with the believers in Jerusalem recognizing God-at-work in what Peter had experienced. God had broken boundaries. God had shown no partiality. God could not be thwarted. God colors outside the lines and runs with scissors. They conclude that God "has given even to the Gentiles the repentance that leads to life" (Acts 11:18), thereby forming a community of Jews *and* Gentiles.

God-at-Work

Remarkable in this narrative concerning Peter and Cornelius is the number of references to God-at-work. Everywhere, the narrative constructs God intervening, directing, guiding, and sanctioning the events. The variety of ways in which God intervenes is extensive:

Acts Passage	Way(s) God Intervenes
10:2-7	prayer, vision, angel
10:9	prayer
10:10-12	trance
10:13-16	voice (3x)
10:17	vision
10:19	vision, the Spirit
10:22	angel

Acts Passage	Way(s) God Intervenes
10:28	vision
10:30-32	prayer, angel
10:33	the presence of God
10:34	vision (implied)
10:35-43	Jesus with Holy Spirit, God
10:44	Holy Spirit
10:45	Holy Spirit
10:47	Holy Spirit
11:1	word of God
11:5	trance, vision
11:7	voice
11:9-10	voice (3x)
11:12	the Spirit
11:13	angel
11:15	Holy Spirit
11:16	word of the Lord, Holy Spirt
11:17	God (2x)
11:18	God

All these references to God's involvement, the repetition through the scene, and its placement in the larger narrative of Acts, emphasize that the inclusion of Gentiles in God's favor is not just the consequence of God-at-work but God's very idea and plan. The scene narrates the key theological perspectives that God has abolished any distinction in creation and among people of clean and profane (10:15, 28), that God shows no partiality for any one group of people (10:34), that God accepts anyone who "fears" or reverences God and "does what is right" (Acts 10:35), that God gives the Spirit to Jew and Gentile alike (Acts 10:45), and that God's work of extending blessing to all cannot be hindered (Acts 11:17). It would be a mistake to think that the inclusion of Gentiles means the exclusion of Jews. God embraces both.

This concentration of central claims about God that justify the inclusion of Gentiles in God's purposes in this scene builds on previous suggestions across Luke-Acts. God's expansive and inclusive purposes are put in the context of God's previous involvements with Gentiles such as Adam and Abraham. Jesus's genealogy goes back to the father of the human family, Adam (Luke 3:38). John the Baptist rejects any appeal to Abraham as the father of Jews only by declaring that God can make even stones into children of Abraham. God is no respecter of ethnic privilege (Luke 3:7-9). Peter explicitly evokes God's promise to Abraham that in his "descendants all the families on earth shall be blessed" (Acts 3:25). Simeon declares Jesus will be "a light for revelation to the Gentiles and for glory to your people Israel" (Luke 2:32). John the Baptist, citing Isaiah 40:5, declares "all flesh shall see the salvation of God" (Luke 3:6). The risen Jesus, God's agent, commissions his followers to preach "to all nations" (Luke 24:47) and sends them as "my witnesses . . . to the end of the earth" (Acts 1:8).

While the Cornelius scene emphasizes divine intrusion and activity, it does so in a context of struggle. Cornelius and Peter struggle to keep up with and understand what God is doing. Cornelius stares in terror at the angel who confronts him in his vision (Acts 10:4). Peter needs to hear three times that God has abolished the distinction of clean and profane and then he is "greatly puzzled about what to make of the vision he had seen" (10:16-17). Two verses later he is "still thinking about" the vision" (10:19). When the Spirit falls on the Gentiles while Peter preaches, the "circumcised [Jewish] believers" were "astounded" (10:45). And the "circumcised believers" in Jerusalem criticized and questioned Peter's behavior (11:3), prompting Peter's thirteen-verse summary of all that had happened. Through these instances, God-at-work challenges these believers as they struggle and conflict with each other in understanding and participating in God-at-work for all people.

But What About . . . ?

The Cornelius-Peter scene celebrates the inclusive and extensive activity of God-at-work. That activity centers on ethnicity in embracing Jewish and Gentile Jesus-believers in one community. But there are some **Red-flag moments** here. What about gender? The women in the households of Cornelius and Peter are invisible in the narrative. And social status?

Cornelius sends household slaves to fetch Peter. These slaves seem to be present when Peter preaches and seem to be included without any say as the household is saved and baptized (Acts 11:14-16). Does God-at-work embrace structures such as social class and gender? And for all its celebration of God's inclusive purposes, what about nonbelievers? Do God's love and purposes embrace them? The **Red flag** is waving.

Social Class

The world of the Roman Empire was very hierarchical. Society comprised, by one count, seven social strata. Three small but graduated strata consisted of wealthy and powerful elites (about 2–3 percent of the population). The remaining four strata comprised various levels of poverty (about 95 percent of society)—those who lived comfortably above subsistence, those who lived around subsistence, those who lived below, and the expendable and broken who, unable to work, struggled for any sort of existence. Luke's Gospel envisions Jesus's ministry as bringing "good news to the poor" (Luke 4:18). Throughout the Gospel, Jesus heals (blind, lame, lepers, deaf), raises the dead, and preaches to the poor (Luke 6:22).

In Acts, however, while these actions continue to occur,[2] they occupy much less space as the narrative unfolds. Poor and broken folks, and powerless and low status people like slaves, so prominent in the Gospel, largely disappear. Preaching and conflicts arising from it increasingly dominate Acts. Apostles like Paul and officials of towns and provinces (folks with power and status) are more prominent. The task of drawing the poor and the broken into God's impartial embrace is unfinished business. The **Red flag** keeps waving.

Gender

The scene involving Peter and Cornelius is very male-centered with two males center stage. The narrative mentions other groups such as Cornelius's "relatives and close friends" (Acts 10:24) and Jewish believers associated with Peter (10:45). If there are women in these groups, the narrative makes them completely invisible. If Acts constructs God as impartial concerning Jews and Gentiles, is the God of Acts impartial concerning women and men? Be ready for a further **Red-flag alert**.

This male-dominated scene is typical of much of Acts. In chapter 1 when the early church gathers, men and women are present (Acts 1:12-13). But while eleven male disciples are named, only one woman has a name, Mary, Jesus's mother. The importance of the men is underlined when only men are considered as replacements for the now-dead Judas in the group of twelve male apostles or leaders (1:15-26). Why are there no women candidates? Thereafter, Peter and Paul dominate the narrative, though there are hints that women are members of the movement (5:14; 8:3; 16:11-15; 17:4, 12, 34; 21:5-6).

> **Five Scenes in Acts Foreground Individual Women**
>
> - A husband and wife, Ananias and **Sapphira,** sell a piece of property (Acts 5:1-11). Both are partners in the decision. They pretend to donate all of the proceeds to the church but withhold some for themselves, thereby deceiving the church, the Holy Spirit, and God. For this deception, they are shockingly struck down dead. The scene is an example story, warning the hearers about deceiving God.
>
> - In the church at Joppa, a woman called **Tabitha** (Dorcas), "devoted to good works and acts of charity," dies (Acts 9:36-43). She is the only woman identified in Acts as a "disciple" (9:36). Her "charity" or almsgiving involves providing clothing for those in need, especially widows. She is a woman with resources who uses them to care for others. Peter revives her.
>
> - **Rhoda** is a female slave belonging to Mary the mother of John Mark (Acts 12:6-17). Mary is a woman of resources. Her gated house has a courtyard large enough for a gathering of Jesus-believers. Peter has just been miraculously freed from prison and comes to Mary's house. Overjoyed to hear Peter's voice at the gate, Rhoda forgets to let him in but reports to the gathering that he is at the gate. They immediately question her sanity ("out of your mind") and suggest she is delusional ("his angel"). Her testimony to God's work is disparaged, and she is offered no apology when they find out she has testified truthfully.

> - Paul visits Philippi and interacts with several women (Acts 16:11-40). He baptizes **Lydia**, a businesswoman dealing in purple cloth, which was especially prized by elites. She provides her home as a base for Paul (16:15). Paul then casts a spirit out of **a slave girl** who practices divination; symbolically, Paul silences her and the narrative pays her no more attention (16:18). Subsequently Paul baptizes the **household of his jailer**, presumably including some women though they are not identified (16:32-34). Lydia's house is mentioned again as a gathering place for Jesus-believers (16:40).
>
> - In Corinth, Paul stays and works with **Priscilla** and Aquila, a Jewish wife and husband team who made tents (Acts 18:1-4). He takes them to Ephesus, but now Priscilla is named before Aquila suggesting some equality in their partnership and prominence for Priscilla. Paul seems to entrust them with some leadership in Ephesus. They instruct Apollos "more accurately" in the "Way of God" (18:26).

What roles do women have in Acts? One role presents widows as recipients of daily food distribution. Some widows from among the Greek-speaking Jews are neglected (Acts 6:1-6). Care for widows was a long-established Jewish practice (Deut 26:12-13), so the church continues this important practice and sets up a means of caring for them. But there are a couple of **Red-flag alerts** in this scene. The practice of providing food relief kept this group of women dependent on the church and under its male control. Moreover, the male apostles are too busy preaching to be concerned about the widows. And further, the solution to the problem of their neglect takes the form of appointing seven *men* to oversee the distribution of food. Women are not empowered for leadership; male-dominated leadership continues. Women are the recipients of the care, but women are not the agents of ministry.

A second role involves women prophets. In Caesarea, four unmarried women, the daughters of an evangelist Philip, "had the gift of prophecy" (Acts 21:9). The narrative does not pause to narrate any of their prophecies. Instead, it turns in the very next verse to a male prophet Agabus and his prophecy concerning Paul's fate in Jerusalem (21:10-14). No other female prophets are mentioned in Acts, nor are there any women apostles. Given the hints of female members in the Jesus communities, we might guess at their types of participation, but the narrative does not make them explicit.

A third role concerns wealthier women who function as patrons or benefactors in using their economic resources to fund the Jesus-movement. Sapphira, along with her husband Ananias, donates to the church some of the proceeds from property they sell (Acts 5:1-11). Mary, the mother of John Mark, has a sizeable house that functions as a gathering place for believers (12:12-17). The businesswoman Lydia in Philippi who sells expensive purple cloth uses her home as a base for Paul and subsequently for the assembly of believers (16:14-15, 40). In Thessalonica, "not a few of the leading women," women of wealth, status, and power, join Paul and Silas (17:4). In Beroea, "not a few Greek women and men of high standing" become believers (17:12). Acts, then, often presents wealthier women as benefactors using their resources to sustain the movement, but it does not present these women as teachers and preachers like the male apostles.

The inequalities in the depiction of women and men in the narrative are clear. Men are far more numerous than the often-invisible women. And men carry out the prominent roles of leadership and proclamation. Women are very much second-class citizens in the Acts narrative. The **Red flag** keeps waving.

The Cornelius story emphasized that "God shows no partiality" to Jewish or Gentile believers. But while Acts has demonstrated God's impartial dealings in regard to ethnicity, it has not been as attentive to nonbelievers, to social class, and to gender. In rendering women and poor folks and making them invisible, the narrative shows a decided partiality toward males and those with resources. There is unfinished business here with regard to God's (im)partiality.

Questions for Reflection/Discussion

1. Summarize the presentations of God in this Cornelius-Peter scene. What do you find significant or plausible?

2. In what ways does the claim that "God shows no partiality" challenge your understandings of God and the practices of your faith community?

3. The discussion identifies three areas of "unfinished business" concerning God's partiality: unbelievers, social status, and gender. What do you think about those discussions? What "unfinished business" concerning God's partiality and impartiality do you see in our world?

Further Reading

Jane Schaberg, "Luke," and Gail O'Day, "Acts," in *Women's Bible Commentary: Expanded Edition with Apocrypha*, ed. Carol Newsom and Sharon Ringe (Louisville: Westminster John Knox, 1998), 363–80; 394–402.

Amy-Jill Levine with Marianne Blickenstaff, eds., *A Feminist Companion to the Acts of the Apostles* (London/New York: Sheffield Academic, 2004).

Chapter 10

God Does Not Play Well with Other Gods (Acts 17:16-34)

> *Read Acts 17:16-34 before reading this chapter. Then refer to it while you read the chapter.*

The biblical writers construct the God of the Bible as a God who does not play well with other gods. Consistently throughout scripture the biblical God is described as a "jealous" God who forbids people worshipping other gods or making idols of them:

> I am the LORD your God, who brought you out of the land of Egypt, out of the house of slavery; you shall have no other gods before me. You shall not make for yourself an idol . . . You shall not bow down to them or worship them; for I the LORD your God, am a jealous God, punishing . . . those who reject me, but showing steadfast love to . . . those who love me and keep my commandments. (Exod 20:2-6)

Why is God so bothered by other gods and idols? Is the biblical tradition arrogant and unyielding in constructing God in this way? Does monotheism by definition promote religious intolerance? Or is there some deeper wisdom for its advocacy of one living God?

The Gods Are Powerless

Psalm 82 at least does not offer a kneejerk response concerning other gods but a considered theological position about them. It proposes some criteria for assessing the worthiness of a god. It presents God accusing the other gods of doing nothing about justice among human beings and showing "partiality to the wicked" (Ps 82:2). God challenges the other gods to "give justice to the weak and the orphan; maintain the right of the lowly and the destitute. Rescue the weak and the needy; deliver them from the hand of the wicked" (Ps 82:3-4).

But the psalm offers no confidence that they can meet the challenge. God condemns them as having "neither knowledge nor understanding" and declares their demise: "you shall die like mortals" (Ps 82:5). That is, the psalm presents these other gods as less than gods because they do not act for justice and lack understanding of the world. They are not worthy constructions of the divine, and they are of no use to most humans (except the powerful wicked). In fact, they sanction human behavior that harms others.

Of course—**Red-flag alert**—the argument can be turned around. One might wonder whether the biblical God might pass God's own test given the ongoing presence of evil and injustice in the world. What or who is a worthy God?

Other biblical texts dismiss idols as human constructs lacking power and understanding. Isaiah 44:9-20 mocks at length the process whereby an ironsmith or a carpenter makes idols, worships what they have made, and begs the idol to act on their behalf. It ridicules idols as being powerless: They "can do no good" (Isa 44:10). The idols "do not know nor do they comprehend: for their eyes are shut, so that they cannot see and their minds . . . cannot understand" (Isa 44:18).

Creating idols results from "a deluded mind [that] has led [their creator] astray"; the idol is a "fraud" (Isa 44:20). Idolatry is condemned because an idol is not a worthy god; it lacks power to act and knowledge to know how to act. In worshipping idols, humans behave in ways that are less than fully human. Ironically, idols have no power yet they exercise enormous power in their creators' lives.

Again the argument might be turned around. Experiences of unanswered prayer and of continuing suffering and misery on our planet might suggest the biblical God does not understand or see or care, despite the claims of passages such as Psalm 139. The **Red flag** is waving.

In Acts 17, Paul offers a different argument about idols. Absent is the mocking that marks these Hebrew Bible passages. He does criticize idols, but the criticism is not mocking, and his tone is generally respectful. His emphasis falls on presenting a positive construction of "the Lord of heaven and earth."

> **The Paul of Acts**
>
> This scene in Acts 17 presents Paul as the speaker. There are significant differences between the presentation of Paul in Acts and in his letters. For starters, the Paul of Acts does not write letters. And it is very difficult to reconcile what Paul says in his letters about his travel plans with the three missionary journeys that Acts constructs for him. There are significant challenges in trying to reconcile Acts 15 (the Jerusalem Council) and Paul's autobiographical account in Galatians 2. Paul in Galatians 2 presents his meeting with the Jerusalem leaders as a private one, not a grand council, and says that the apostles "contributed nothing" (Gal 2:6). Acts 15 presents James sending a postcouncil letter to the believers in Antioch, Syria, and Cilicia, setting out four requirements for Gentile believers (Acts 15:23-29). Paul does not mention James's letter in his letters and says that they wanted Gentile believers to do only one thing (to remember the poor), which he was happy to do (Gal 2:10). Further, there are significant differences in the theology of Paul's speeches in Acts and that of his letters. A major concern in the letters—that God effects justification through Jesus's death "for us" (Rom 3:24-26; 5:6-11)—receives little attention in Acts. Likewise, while Paul is repeatedly insistent on the return of Jesus to establish God's purposes in full, Acts pays little attention to this theme.
>
> These differences suggest that the writer of Acts has taken significant liberties in constructing his image of Paul some fifty or so years after Paul's activity. I will refer to Paul throughout the rest of this chapter in the sense of the Paul presented in Acts.

Paul in Athens

The scene sets Paul in Athens (Acts 17:16). In Paul's time, Athens was not a large city, but it remained a city of great culture, an intellectual center with a distinguished past marked by philosophy and rhetoric. The great Roman orator, Cicero, had trained there. It was also a city renowned for its idols and statues. Here Paul encounters tolerant and diverse Athenian philosophy, wisdom, and polytheistic culture.

Acts 17:16 describes the reaction of the Jewish, monotheistic Paul to this city of idols. He is "deeply distressed" or "angry" or "provoked to wrath." This verb, though, expresses more than Paul's response. The verb is commonly used in the Greek version of the Hebrew Bible, the Septuagint, to describe God's anger against Israel for engaging in idolatrous worship (Deut 9:7-8, 18-19; Ps 106:28-29). Paul's response expresses God's point of view. Monotheism rejects idolatrous polytheism.

Paul, though, does not turn his back on the city. He seems to swallow his anger. Instead, he engages the city and its polytheistic culture, debating first with Jewish folks in the synagogue and Athenians in the marketplace (Acts 17:17) and then with Epicurean and Stoic philosophers. Among philosophical groups, the Epicureans were commonly regarded as "impious" or, in our terms, secular. They denied the gods, rejected popular worship practices involving sacrifices, and did not fear death because they denied any afterlife of retribution. Stereotypically, they sought to avoid pain with a commitment to pleasure. They were commonly accused of hedonism and atheism.

Stoic thought was much more widespread in popular culture. They saw pleasure more commonly as a vice. They affirmed the gods, often in personal terms, as caring for human needs. They also understood a divine principle or logos to govern the cosmos.

Paul's initial preaching focuses on God raising Jesus from the dead. Neither the Epicureans nor Stoics are impressed. One group, perhaps the Epicureans, declare Paul to be a "babbler" (Acts 17:18). The word uses the image of a bird randomly picking up seeds or scraps from the ground, suggesting that as a teacher, Paul gathers scraps from others. It insults Paul as guilty of, variously, plagiarism or incoherency. Another group, perhaps

God Does Not Play Well with Other Gods (Acts 17:16-34)

the Stoics, is less hostile, labeling Paul a "proclaimer of foreign divinities" (Acts 17:18).

These folks take Paul to the Areopagus council (Acts 17:19-21). This council, comprising leading Athenian citizens, had responsibility for any aspect of Athenian life including education, foreign religious groups, philosophical teaching, public morality, and criminal trials. Acts 17:19b-20 suggests they are taking their civic oversight responsibilities seriously by checking out Paul's teaching ("May we know . . . it sounds rather strange to us . . ."). And verse 21's description of them spending their time "telling or hearing something new" suggests an openness to new teaching in the city.

So in Acts 17:22-31, Paul makes a presentation to the council. He begins with an ambiguous compliment about the idols and altars he has seen in the city (17:22-23a). He announces his intention to make known to them the "unknown god" to whom they have dedicated an altar (17:23b). He then makes his argument in terms of God as the creator, governor, and sustainer of the earth and human existence (17:24-29). He concludes with an appeal representing God's demand for people to repent in the light of an upcoming day of judgment carried out "by a man whom" God has raised from the dead (17:30-31).

Throughout, Paul frequently echoes philosophical teachings. But central to his proclamation are biblical traditions about Israel's God. He mentions God explicitly five times. He identifies their "unknown god" with Israel's God (Acts 17:23), the creator of the world (17:24), for whom people should search (17:27) since "we are God's offspring" or children of a God (17:29) who calls people to repent (17:30). These five explicit references to God frame the whole passage and focus on Paul's construction of God in relation to idols.

Paul begins by observing "I see how extremely religious you are in every way" (Acts 17:22). It's an ambiguous statement about the many idols that he had observed and that had angered him in Athens. The ambiguity comes in the adjective translated "religious." Normally we would expect a compliment, not an insult, at the opening of a speech as the speaker seeks to connect with the audience, gain their favor, and arouse their interest.

The term would, then, normally be positive with the meaning of "pious," or "devout."

But the term can also be used negatively to mean "superstitious" or "fearful" in denoting untrustworthy or mean gods. Perhaps here the positive meaning is to the fore since Paul will build off their practice of worshipping idols, but the negative cannot be ruled out given his initial anger about the many idols (Acts 17:22) and his final appeal to repent from idol worship (17:30).

He then zooms in on one particular altar dedicated "to an unknown god" (Acts 17:23). Such altars for "unknown" or "anonymous" gods were common in ancient cities. In a polytheistic context, one could never be sure to have honored all deities. To not honor a deity runs the risk of a deity bringing disaster (such as famine, disease, misfortune in love or business, or warfare) upon an individual, household, city, or nation.

Paul declares his intention: "What therefore you worship as unknown, this I proclaim to you" (Acts 17:23). The first part of the sentence emphasizes the Athenians' worship of an "unknown" deity; the second part focuses on Paul's proclamation or revelation as to the identity of this deity.

Paul now elaborates his claim. He focuses on God-at-work in creation and in relation to human beings. This God is not distant and remote, unknowable and mysterious, says Paul. Rather, this God is involved in everything, up close, and personal. Paul employs ideas known in Greek philosophy but draws from Israel's traditions to define this knowable God. Paul makes ten claims.

First, Paul begins where the biblical tradition begins, with the claim from Genesis 1:1–2:4 that God "made the world and everything in it, he is Lord of heaven and earth" (Acts 17:24; also Exod 20:11; Isa 42:5). As such, the creator has proprietary rights over "heaven and earth" as its "Lord" or sovereign. This creation, in turn, points to the creator. People could comprehend something about God as the creator from observing creation. The notions that the supreme deity (known as Zeus) was creator of the material world and could be known from it were familiar to Greek philosophers. Paul, though, does not explicitly appeal to this argument here.

Inherent in Paul's claim about God is another claim, one concerning people. The claim that God created everything constructs humans as creatures. Humans come into being at God's pleasure, dependent on and accountable to this sovereign-creator God. Paul's construction of God, then, has important implications for his understanding of human identity and lifestyle.

Second, Paul asserts that God "does not live in shrines or temples made by human hands." (Acts 17:24). This assertion follows from the previous one. A God who made and rules heaven and earth cannot be confined by a temple built by humans. The idea is expressed in biblical literature (1 Kgs 8:27; Isa 66:1-2) as well as in various philosophers.[1] Again Paul draws on his biblical tradition as well as commonly recognized philosophical insights to build common ground while also stating his particular truth. His claim carries an implicit critique of all the temples and their gods in Athens.

Third, Paul declares that God is not served "by human hands, as though he needed anything" (Acts 17:25a). The one who made everything and is sovereign over all needs nothing. Again Paul bridges Greek philosophy and biblical understandings. God's self-sufficiency was recognized in Greek philosophical thought. In fact, some viewed the supreme God as so remote and distant that God was unfeeling and not moved by what happened on earth. Others rejected this view of God's lack of feeling or impassability (as it was known). They affirmed the value of prayer and sacrifices, along with divine care for the suffering. While God does not need human worship, others argued, God merits such honoring. The biblical tradition conveys some similar understandings. The prophet Isaiah has Israel's God rejecting offerings and prayers, not because God does not care, but because God wants them to be accompanied by just and caring actions: "learn to do good; seek justice, rescue the oppressed, defend the orphan, plead for the widow" (Isa 1:11-17; also Ps 50:7-15). God responds to prayer because God lovingly and generously provides more than a person needs (Luke 11:8-13).

Fourth, while God is self-sufficient and needs nothing, God reaches out to creation to "give life and breath and all things" (Act 17:25). The thought returns to the creation story of God giving breath to humans (Gen 2:7). But it extends beyond the act of creation to recognize that God sustains the world God created.

Fifth, Paul moves from God-at-work in creating and sustaining the world to God-at-work with humanity. "From one ancestor he made all nations to inhabit the whole earth" (Acts 17:26). Again there are points of intersection with Hellenistic philosophy. And again Paul evokes the creation story by referring to Adam as the ancestor of all people (the Greek form is masculine; Gen 2:7). The common origin of all humanity underscores God's sovereignty over all creation and people, God's favor on all people,[2] and human accountability to God, a theme Paul will emphasize in Acts 17:30-31.

Sixth, God-at-work structures the human world. God "allotted the times of their existence and the boundaries of the places where they would live" (Acts 17:26b). God's organization of (or sovereignty over) time and space is evidenced in the creation story with God dividing night from day, the heavens from the earth, and the dry land from the sea (Gen 1). God's sovereignty also extends over the nations (Gen 10). God chooses Israel from among the nations to witness to the nations (Isa 42:1-9). God uses empires to accomplish God's purposes. So, for example, God anoints the Persian ruler Cyrus to set free God's people from exile in Babylon and return them to their land (Isa 44:28–45:1). God measures out the times of the rise and fall of empires. In Daniel 7, the Babylonians, Medes, Persians, and Greeks come and go in accord with God's purposes. The implication is that the dominant contemporary empire (Rome) will undergo a similar fate and be subject to God's designs, whatever the current situation of its unchallengeable supremacy seems to suggest (see Luke 1:51-54).

Seventh, up to this point, Paul has constructed a powerful God-at-work in creation and international affairs. One might conclude from this that God, who is Lord of heaven and earth, who needs nothing from humans, and who directs nations is distant and remote with little interest in individuals. Verse 27 counters this impression. "Indeed he is not far from each one of us," says Paul (Acts 17:27). The language of "each one of us" is individual, personal, and relational in affirming God's nearness to all people. Paul denies that his deity is "foreign" or disinterested in Athenians/Gentiles (17:21).

In what way is God near? Paul quotes a Greek poet (perhaps a sixth-century BCE Cretan poet Epimenides): "In him we live and move and have our being" (17:28). The translation of "in him" could also read "by him"; the first translation suggests God as the environment or habitat in which humans live; the second suggests God's presence and agency at work in the midst of the human world. Whichever option we choose (or both), verse 27 emphasizes that humans are to "search . . . grope for . . . and find" this God who is near. But the adverb "perhaps" and traditions from the scriptures in which searching has not led to encounter with God (Wis 3:5-9) do not guarantee success. Divine revelation requires, but is not contained by, human questing.

Eighth, Paul continues the thought. God is not far from human beings because we humans are God's offspring/family/children (Acts 17:28), bearing God's image (Acts 17:29). Again he builds bridges with his audience by quoting another poet, the third-century BCE Greek poet Aratus: "for we too are his offspring." That Zeus or Jupiter was the father of humanity was a philosophical commonplace, and Paul evokes Jewish traditions in which God is Israel's father. Here in verses 26-27, though, he has a much wider focus. The noun "image" in verse 29 recalls the creation story in which God creates *all* human beings in God's image (Gen 1:26-27).

Ninth, Paul denies that this God can be represented in idols (Acts 17:29). This claim logically follows the previous verse. If humans are God's offspring or children, God cannot be the offspring or creation of humans! Here he builds on a long biblical tradition (and some Greek philosophical writers also) that critiqued idols or human representations of the gods (Deut 7:15; 29:17). Gold, silver, stone, artistic representations, and human imagination cannot do justice to the one who created the world.

And tenth, and perhaps most controversially for his audience, Paul constructs God as the one to whom they are accountable and who requires their repentance. Paul has built common ground throughout, but now any sense of compromise or tolerance disappears. Paul makes his appeal for repentance urgent by pointing out that the time of God's patience for human ignorance has expired. Calling the cultured and learned Athenians ignorant is not especially smart even if Paul's point is that God does not want people to continue in ignorance of God.

Paul has revealed God-at-work in creating and governing the world and in being near to people. But there is a further revelation of God. There is a day coming that God has fixed for judgment. And God has appointed an unnamed man as its agent or judge (Acts 17:31). To appoint a man to judge the world is most unusual, so God offers assurance or proof in raising him from the dead. The lack of the use of Jesus's name suggests the emphasis is more theological—on God-at-work in effecting judgment—than christological—in identifying the agent. Paul asserts God's resurrection of Jesus but offers no explanation apart from credentialing Jesus to act on God's behalf in judging the world.

The scene ends with three responses: some mock the notion of resurrection, some express interest in hearing more, and some become believers. By building on Greek philosophical insights throughout, Paul has recognized human culture as providing helpful pointers toward God. He does not disrespect or dismiss that culture, even as the scene shows that further proclamation is necessary and that many remain unconvinced by Paul's bridge-building.

Questions for Reflection/Discussion

1. How does Paul deal with other gods? Can people be persuaded of God's existence and nature? If so, how? What does or does not persuade you?

2. Numerous biblical texts make a case against idolatry and polytheism. In addition to the texts cited above (Ps 82; Isa 44:9-20), what arguments are made in Psalm 115, Isaiah 46:1-7, Jeremiah 10:1-16, Wisdom of Solomon 13:10–15:17, and 1 Corinthians 8:1-6? Are these convincing arguments and how might they address contemporary idols (identify some) constructed in our society? Do idols render us less than human? If so, how?

God Does Not Play Well with Other Gods (Acts 17:16-34)

3. Is monotheism by definition religiously arrogant and intolerant in claiming only one God? How might Christian monotheism interact with other monotheisms (Judaism, Islam)?

4. Paul's ten claims about God could be read like a creed: "I believe in God who created . . ." Reconstruct Paul's possible creed about God from the ten claims above. What would *your* "creed" about God be?

Further Reading

Neil Richardson, *Who on Earth Is God? Making Sense of the Bible* (New York: Bloomsbury, 2014).

Chapter 11

God Doesn't Throw Thunderbolts (Rom 1:16-32)

> *Read Romans 1:16-32 before reading the chapter. Then refer to it while you read the chapter.*

Paul, whose letters are the earliest writings in the New Testament, is not everybody's favorite person. He has always been controversial and difficult to understand. The writer of 2 Peter says: "So also our beloved brother Paul wrote to you . . . There are some things in them hard to understand which the ignorant and unstable twist to their own destruction (2 Pet 3:15-16).

Several factors account for these difficulties in his letters. One is that Paul is a complex thinker. He thinks "big," even cosmically, about God-at-work in the world. Yet he also thinks "local." In Romans, he addresses the circumstances of local Jesus-believers in Rome in the light of God's "big" purposes. That combination can make him tough for outsiders to decipher.

Paul's language presents another challenge. Paul thinks about God in terms of images that he draws from both the Hebrew Bible and from his cultural context. Terms such as *salvation*, or *faith/fullness* or *righteousness* or *wrath* are examples. For Paul's readers, these are familiar images, but for us as cultural outsiders, reading cross-culturally some two thousand years later, the images are often strange even when we think we are familiar with the language. Language picks up different meanings across the millennia. We have to stop and think about the meaning of Paul's language.

In Paul's letter to the churches in Rome, the capital of the Roman Empire, Paul addresses a situation of conflict. Chapters 14–15 show that at its center the conflict concerns relationships between Jewish Jesus-believers and Gentile Jesus-believers. Up for grabs is the issue of how people belong to communities of Jesus-believers, or in bigger terms, how people participate in God's purposes. Are particular practices or spiritualities like Sabbath and food purity necessary? Or the reverse, does observance of these spiritualities or practices prevent membership and participation? Paul's approach is to elaborate the big picture of God's purposes that embrace Jews and Gentiles before addressing their specific conflicts. He spells out the big picture so that his readers can understand their own situation and behave appropriately in the light of the big picture.

The Good News: Romans 1:16-17

Interpreters have long regarded these two verses as a summary of or thesis statement for Paul's argument for the whole of Romans. The first thing to notice is that the two verses are about God. He does not mention Jesus. He began the letter talking about the "gospel of God" (1:1), addressing the letter to "all God's beloved in Rome" (1:7), declaring he serves God (1:9), and evoking God's will (1:10). Now he describes God's big plans for the world. We can describe Paul, at least in this section of Romans, as a theocentric, rather than Christocentric, thinker.

A second thing to notice about Romans 1:16-17 is the tone of the two verses. Paul is very confident, very upbeat. "I'm not ashamed of the gospel," he declares (1:16). By using the negative "not" and the verb "ashamed," he makes an understatement (*litotes*) that is actually very emphatic. "I am very proud of the gospel." "I am most confident in the gospel."

What does he mean by "gospel" or "good news" (as it could be translated)?[1] He is not referring to the written documents of Matthew, Mark, Luke, and John. They were not written yet. Nor, as the next clause in verse 16 shows, is he referring to just words, a creed or confession that sums up some doctrinal content. Rather, he is referring to God-at-work. "It [the gospel] is," Paul says, "the power of God-at-work into salvation/safety/wholeness." He emphasizes the effect of the gospel or good news. It is dynamic. It empowers people. It takes hold of their lives. It comprises the power of God-at-work moving people and the world into salvation or safety.

What is this salvation/safety/wholeness? These different translation options show that it is a tricky word. In contemporary religious jargon, the word often refers to getting right with God, having one's sins forgiven and one's soul saved so that one will go to heaven instead of hell. This use of the word refers to an experience that is personal, spiritual, individual, and internal.

This meaning, though, does not fit with the circumstances of Paul writing to a *social-ecclesial* situation comprising conflicted churches of Jesus-believers living in the center of the Roman Empire. Paul wants reconciliation between these Jewish and Gentile believers whereby both groups recognize the legitimacy of the other in God's purposes regardless of their different practices. His claim is that God-at-work can power them through their prejudices and animosities into reconciled relationships. Salvation, then, is partly a social experience of reconciliation that results from, participates in, and enacts God's inclusive and powerful purposes.

But subsequently in the letter Paul elaborates another element of salvation—a cosmic dimension. Paul understands the world to be in the grips of another power, namely the power of sin. Under this power, the world is heading to divine judgment that will end the present age and its destructive powers. Paul thinks in terms of two ages or periods of time. The present age of Roman rule is dominated by sin, evil, and death. A coming new age will see the establishment of God's rule or good purposes in full for all people. In this two-age scenario, salvation means being rescued or saved from the powers at work in the present evil age and entrance into the fullness of God's purposes for human beings and all God's creation. Salvation, then, is not a spiritual escape but an entrance into a new physical, corporeal world under God's gracious rule. The word refers to cosmic safety and wholeness.

These two dimensions of God's saving power at work are interrelated. The local or social dimension of God-at-work empowers the conflicted Jewish and Gentile Jesus-believers to reconcile with each other because they recognize that God's cosmic purposes involve the inclusion of all people in a re-created world. Their reconciliation participates in, prepares for, and anticipates God's cosmic work that God has still to complete. This is the cosmic "bigness" of God's purposes that is experienced in local communities. God's power moving people and the world into salvation combines local and cosmic dimensions.

In Romans 1:17, Paul rolls out another image for God-at-work. The emphasis on power gives way to a focus on faithfulness. Just as the gospel exhibits power for salvation, so it also reveals God's "righteousness" or "justice" at work. How does it do so?

The word *righteousness* is not one we commonly use. It sounds old-fashioned and a little stuffy, to be honest. And when we think of justice, we often think of people getting their just desserts and appropriate punishment. To bring someone to justice, or to declare that justice was done in a particular situation, enacts this idea. None of this, though, is helpful for understanding Paul's language. He draws on several important Hebrew Bible ideas.

The first of these ideas is that the words translated as *righteousness* are primarily relational terms. *Righteousness* consists of behaving in the right way in accord with the expectations of a relationship and in the eyes of another. It refers to doing the right thing by another. To be righteous is to be the person who is acknowledged by another to have behaved in the right way, to have done the right thing expected in the relationship. Words like *faithful* and *just* are appropriate synonyms. To act righteously is to act *faithfully* or *justly*.

The second of these ideas concerns God-at-work being righteous or behaving righteously. God behaves righteously or displays righteousness when God acts faithfully to the expectations of God's covenant relationship with Israel. Isaiah 42:6 declares God's commitment to a faithful, righteous relationship with Israel, which is expressed in God delivering the people from captivity in Babylon. In fact, Isaiah 40–55 frequently translates the word *righteousness* as *deliverance* (Isa 46:13) or *salvation* (Isa 51:5-6). These translations express the notion that *righteousness* refers to God-at-work, God-in-action faithfully, justly, or righteously delivering or saving the people from dominating empires.

Paul builds on these ideas in 1:17 and throughout Romans. He argues that God not only continues to act righteously or faithfully to the covenant relationship with Israel ("to the Jew first"). God also—as the creator of the world—acts faithfully or righteously for all creation thereby embracing Gentiles as well. In so doing, God works to bring all people into right relationship with God. Paul says subsequently that even human faithlessness or sinfulness cannot negate God's faithful activity (Rom 3:3). God-at-work is powerful and faithful.

Paul then identifies a further crucial dimension of God acting righteously. God's righteousness is revealed, Paul says, "through faith for faith." A literal translation reads "out of faith/faithfulness into faith/faithfulness." Again we have an English translation problem—is it *faith* or *faithfulness*? What is Paul referring to? Why use these prepositions "out of" and "into"?

Paying attention to the context and meaning of *righteousness* and Paul's choice of prepositions points to another statement about God-at-work. The revelation of God-acting-righteously begins in God's faithfulness to God's identity as creator of the world and commitments to just and life-giving human interactions. Faithfulness is expressed in actions, so when God acts faithfully, it has an impact among people: "from [God's] faithfulness into [human] faithfulness." God acting righteously or faithfully powers people—Jews and Gentiles—into a right or faithful relationship with God. People act or live faithfully to this relationship with God by also living or acting righteously or faithfully with other human beings. God's action sparks the changes in behavior Paul wants among the believers in Rome (the local), which is part of what God is doing in the whole world (the cosmic). God's initiative powers faithful or righteous human response. He seals the argument by citing a verse from Habakkuk (Hab 2:4).

There's a **Red-flag alert**. Paul makes it sound so triumphant as though God inevitably effects these changes, but humans and human society have so often proven very resistant to this divine power.

Now the Bad News: The Antithesis (Rom 1:18-32)

Paul's declaration of the good news of God acting powerfully and faithfully among all people for salvation/safety/wholeness assumes a need for God to act in this way. Why is that so? What circumstances require God to act this way? The point Paul will make in Romans 3:20 is that God acting powerfully and faithfully is necessary because people need rescuing or saving from another power—that of sin: "For 'no human being will be justified in his sight' by deeds prescribed by the law, for through the law comes the knowledge of sin" (3:20).

Paul begins his exposé of sin's enslaving power in Romans 1:18-32 by taking up one aspect: the practice of idolatry. As we observed in the last chapter's discussion of Acts 17 and Paul's presentation before the Areopagus council, there is a long Jewish tradition of revulsion for idols. Jewish rejection of idols was a distinctive marker of Israel's identity (along with Sabbath observance, food purity, and circumcision) that separated Jewish folks from Gentiles. The Paul of Acts 17 critiques the idolatry of Athens with some gentleness, explains it as belonging to a time of human ignorance, and then calls his audience to repent (Acts 17:30). Here in Romans 1:18-32, however, Paul is much more aggressive, refuses to excuse the practice ("they are without excuse," 1:20) and strongly condemns its practitioners.

Paul frames his discussion in terms of "the wrath of God" that is revealed against human "ungodliness and wickedness" (1:18). This language of "wrath" suggests to us a very angry deity hurling down thunderbolts at any and every human who has irritated him! Paul's view, however, is somewhat different even if it is not a particularly endearing construction of God. He draws on Hebrew Bible traditions that understand negative or disastrous events as the consequences of people turning their backs on God and therefore dishonoring God. So in Psalm 78, the psalmist rehearses the story of Israel from the exodus to David's kingship. Several times, the psalm notes the people's disobedience that provokes God's wrath or anger to be displayed in an act of revenge or seeking satisfaction:

> But before they had satisfied their craving, while the food was still in their mouths, the anger of God rose against them and he killed the strongest of them, and laid low the flower of Israel (Ps 78:30-31; also 78:21)

God Doesn't Throw Thunderbolts (Rom 1:16-32)

This is not an endearing construction of God in killing Israel's youth for disobedience! The psalm also presents the plagues against Egypt as expressions of God's wrath (78:43-51, esp. 78:49). Yet it also indicates God is not out of control; God can, apparently, restrain God's wrath (78:38). Elsewhere, in Isaiah 10:5-6, Assyria's invasion of Israel is interpreted as an expression of God's anger against the sinful people. Often, then, disastrous national or individual events are interpreted as displays of God's wrath in which God takes satisfaction in an act of revenge for being dishonored by the people.

The texts are consistent in showing that God is not fickle or vindictive in such displays. God is not just having a moment. God's wrath seeks satisfaction for being dishonored and does so in disasters that result when humans rebel against God. This claim, though, is very problematic, and the **Red flag** is waving. It's an appalling case of "blame the victim." They brought it on themselves! They deserved the revenge! They made God do it. God is just having to do what God has to do! Blaming the victim, though, often tries to hide the responsibility of the one committing the violent action, but there's no disguising God's agency in this scenario.

Paul goes on to claim that people who rebel against God with ungodliness and wickedness "suppress the truth" (Rom 1:18). What truth? The following verses interweave two emphases. The truth about God as creator is suppressed in favor of false worship of creatures (idols). And the truth about people as God's creatures created to live in faithful relationship with God is suppressed in favor of unrighteous actions—that which is unfaithful to or not right in relationship to God ("a debased mind and things that should not be done;" 1:28).

Paul is clear that humans can know about God from the created world. Three times in Romans 1:19-20 Paul refers to God making Godself known in creation. This knowledge is "plain"; "God has shown it to them"; and God can be "understood and seen through the things he has made." Particularly, God has revealed or made visible God's power and divine nature. Paul concludes people are "without excuse."

Having established the availability of this knowledge, Paul now intensifies the condemnation (Rom 1:21-23). People ignore what they know about God and so do not honor or give thanks to God. It is a matter of the will, of choosing not to act on their knowledge. By not honoring or giving thanks to God, they turn away from God and deny their own identity as God's creatures.

This denial leads to distorted and foolish thinking to not glorify God—which means not recognizing God's power and presence. Idols result. Idolatry reflects a distorted and perverted perception of reality that does not recognize the creator God. Paul calls them fools for giving their allegiance to "images resembling mortal human being or birds or four-footed animals or reptiles" (Rom 1:23). Their foolishness means turning the natural order of creator and creature on its head. Creatures now become creators who worship their creatures. At root is the denial of God's existence and creative power. "Fools say in their hearts, 'there is no God'" (Ps 14:1).

God responds with wrath to this dishonoring. How is this wrath expressed? Three times in the next eight verses, Paul declares that God's wrath is expressed not with thunderbolts, not with punitive international disasters, but by a different approach: "God gave them up" or "God handed them over" (Rom 1:24, 26, 28). God's response is to respect these human decisions and let people experience the consequences of their decisions.

Paul offers three examples of God "giving up" people to the consequences of their distorted thinking and choices. The first example concerns lustful hearts, impurity, and degrading bodily behaviors (Rom 1:24-25). We think immediately of sexually immoral behaviors, but Paul's reference probably denotes any behaviors that ignore divine purposes. In Gal 5:19-21, Paul offers a catalogue of such behaviors: fornication, impurity, licentiousness, idolatry, sorcery, enmities, strife, jealousy, anger, quarrels, dissensions, factions, envy, drunkenness, carousing, and things like these.

How does this lifestyle express God's wrath, especially when some of these behaviors can be understood to be good fun? Paul's point is that anything that dishonors the creature-creator relationship means people live in ways contrary to God's purposes.

Paul's second example of God "giving up" people to the consequences of their distorted thinking and choices concerns "degrading passions."

God Doesn't Throw Thunderbolts (Rom 1:16-32)

Romans 1:26-27 has been very controversial, especially in contemporary debates about same-sex relationships and marriage. Some interpret the verses as expressing God's displeasure against all and any same-sex interaction. Some understanding, though, of gender roles in the ancient world suggests Paul is talking about particular constructions of same-sex relationships, notably those of unequal power relations (such as a master and slave) or pederasty (a form of child abuse), that differ from contemporary constructions of loving and mutual interactions.

Paul begins by condemning "females [who] traded natural sexual relations for unnatural sexual relations" (Rom 1:26). Often this is understood as a reference to same-sex or lesbian relationships, but Paul does not explicitly say so. Natural intercourse for women in the ancient world usually meant sex to get pregnant. "Unnatural intercourse" meant sex for pleasure or sex in which the woman played the dominant and active role.

Romans 1:27, by comparison, explicitly refers to same-sex relationships involving men. In the ancient world, the dominant form of male same-sex relationships involved an older male and a younger male, perhaps a friend's son or a slave or prostitute. In this interaction, the older male assumed the more active role; the younger male played the passive role of a penetrated woman. This latter role was widely regarded as dishonorable for a male. The interaction was exploitative, an abuse of power, and of course, it could not do what natural sex was understood to do, namely produce children. Public opinion was divided about this form of same-sex relationships. Paul joins those who disapprove.

It is important to notice that Paul discusses here particular forms of same-sex relationships that dominated the ancient world. He is not talking about the loving, committed, mutual same-sex relationships of our world. He is not talking about same-sex marriage. How Paul would view these expressions of same-sex interactions we do not know.

Paul's third example of God "giving up" people to the consequences of their distorted thinking and choices widens the focus considerably but makes the same point. Romans 1:28-31 suggests all hell breaks loose when people ignore the knowledge of God revealed in creation. With the violation of the central creator-creature relationship, the rest of the social order and human interactions comes under threat. So he mentions a range of behaviors that disrupts and destroys civil social interactions and relationships: "covetousness, malice, envy, murder, strife, deceit, craftiness . . . gossips, slanderers, insolent . . . rebellious toward parents . . . heartless, ruthless," among others. Such behaviors harm others. Not only do people live this way, they "applaud others who practice" these behaviors.

In Romans 1:18-32, Paul has outlined the sort of world that requires God to act powerfully and faithfully to rescue or save the world of Jews and Gentiles—including the groups among the believers in Rome in conflict with each other. When the foundational creator-creature relationship is breached by people choosing not to heed "what can be known about God" (Rom 1:19) and instead creating their own gods, the dishonored God gives people up to the consequences of their choices. These consequences involve not thunderbolts but behaviors that are self-destructive and destructive to social order and human interaction. And God acts in such circumstance to rescue or save the world, says Paul.

Questions for Reflection/Discussion

1. Check out Paul's vocabulary in this passage. How does he use these words in the passage: *gospel* (discussed in ch. 4 on Mark 1:15), *salvation, faith/fullness, righteousness*, and *wrath*?

2. Why is he so opposed to idols? Compare with chapter 10's discussion of Acts 17. Identify some contemporary idols. Does Paul's critique apply to them and us?

3. Some have seen Wisdom of Solomon 13–16 as an important influence on Paul's thinking. Read those chapters. What critique of idolatry do they offer and how does this compare with Romans 1:18-32?

4. If God's revelation happens though creation, how do we interpret humanity's dominion over and exploitation of the created world?

Chapter 12
God's Love Wins? (Rom 8:31-39; 11:25-32)

> *Read Romans 8:31-39; 11:25-32 before reading the chapter. Then refer to them while you read the chapter. This chapter builds on the discussion of Romans 1:16-32 in the previous chapter. It would be a good idea to read that chapter before this one.*

In discussing Romans 1:16-32 in the last chapter, I pointed out that Paul constructs God primarily in terms of power and righteousness or faithfulness. His claim is that God acts powerfully and faithfully in the face of human sinfulness and faithlessness to execute God's purposes to bring all people—Jews and Gentiles—into faithful relationship with God.

We need to pause, though, to think about this scenario. Having power and acting faithfully to one's purposes is not necessarily positive. Tyrants from Alexander the Great to the emperor Augustus to Adolf Hitler have acted powerfully, been faithful to their visions of world domination, and sought by numerous violent means to draw all people under their rule. Crime families, gangsters, the mafia, and neighborhood, workplace, and playground bullies have also had power and visions of domination to which they have acted faithfully—and cruelly. What, if anything, makes God different? What, if anything, makes Paul's presentation persuasive?

In the sections from Romans chapters 8 and 11 that I discuss in this chapter, Paul adds another layer to his construction of God in Romans. In addition to power and faithfulness, Paul's God specializes in love and mercy. God-at-work acts powerfully, faithfully/righteously, *and* with love and mercy. What does this love and mercy look like?

Both Jewish and non-Jewish traditions speak of people being embraced by the love of a god or gods. The psalmist speaks of God rescuing those whom God loves (Pss 60:5; 108:6). So Paul's claim is not unique. Yet for Paul, God's love has several distinctive dimensions. To speak of God's love is to talk of God-at-work in the community of Jesus's believers, in the death of Jesus, and in the whole cosmos.

Paul begins his letter by greeting the Jesus-believers in Rome as "God's beloved" or "the ones loved by God" (Rom 1:7). He attaches the word "all" to this greeting to emphasize that these believers who include both Jews and Gentiles are embraced in God's inclusive love. It's powerful enough to form communities that are rooted in and caught up in the experience of God's love.

Inquiring minds, of course, want to know, though, how Paul knows that God displays such powerful love. After all, countless numbers of human lives across the ages do not seem to have experienced such love in their lives and circumstances. Rather than love, many like the biblical Job have experienced themselves as cursed or neglected by God, not loved. How does Paul know?

In Romans 5, Paul turns to a historical event and says, "There's the supreme demonstration!" At first blush, his choice of proof seems strange and disturbing. Wave the **Red flag**.

Paul points to the death of Jesus on a Roman cross as the sign of how much God loves all people (Rom 5:6-11). Of course, when the Roman governor Pilate crucified Jesus around the year 30 CE, some twenty-five or so years before Paul writes to the church in Rome, no one thought Jesus's God-forsaken death on a cross was about love.[1] There were no neon lights, parades, or bumper stickers. Quite the opposite. As a form of the death penalty, crucifixion was a horribly painful and shameful way to die. It was a form of punishment that Roman elites regarded as so shameful

God's Love Wins? (Rom 8:31-39; 11:25-32)

and painful that they reserved it for poor folks, rebellious provincials, and slaves. Folks didn't get crucified for saying their prayers. They got crucified for threatening imperial rule and structures. First came torture with whipping and mocking; then came death. Crucifixions were public. They enacted a clear message of rejection. Such folks were not welcome in the Roman world.

Why would Paul put a sticky note on this brutal and torturous event of crucifixion that says, "God loves you"? This violent execution is a long way from our conventional expressions of love. Think Valentine's Day, heart-shaped boxes of chocolates, red roses, and special dinners. Paul's claim is shocking.

But perhaps that's its point. It certainly gets our attention. It's so contrary to what we expect. Paul reframes an event of torture, pain, rejection, and death to re-present it as an event of God-at-work that displays God's inclusive love. He re-presents an event of death, defeat, and weakness as a triumph of loving power. God's love extends, apparently, even this far to an unwanted, rejected criminal. God's love embraces one who is rejected by the ruling elite as a threat to their society. God's love is displayed in someone whom society has rejected as beyond the acceptable. God does not wait for people to "scrub up nice," to wash their hair, and put on their makeup and cute clothes. God takes the initiative in reaching out in love even to the furthermost margins. "While we were still weak . . . ungodly . . . sinners, God proves his love for us . . . Christ died for us" (Rom 5:6-8). To be classified as ungodly and sinners are hardly CV-leading, attention-getting credentials—except for Paul's loving God. Out there on the margins, even among the unlovely and weak, God-at-work is encountered—in love.

Is God's love displayed in Jesus's death confined to the dim distant past? Paul says no. "And hope does not disappoint us, because God's love has been poured into our hearts through the Holy Spirit that has been given to us" (Rom 5:5). The sort of love displayed in Jesus's death continues to be known among people because God is at work through the Holy Spirit.

Is all of this too good to be true? Paul doesn't think so. He declares God loves "for us," for our benefit, for our gain. God is turned toward humans. Paul elaborates these benefits by talking of God's present and future actions. God's welcoming love sets people in right relation with God, reconciles enemies, and makes them into friends. And, changing tenses, God's love will rescue or save people in the coming age from God's wrath (Rom 5:9-10). God's love powerfully woos people into this new life.

But again we need to be careful. It's a pity to fly the **Red flag** again and pop the balloon, but there is an unpleasant side to Paul's claim. The man whose crucifixion displays the love of God, according to Paul, is God's son, Jesus (Rom 5:10). Paul understands God to give his own son to die "for us." What sort of father, what sort of God, gives up his own son to die a brutal and terrible death at the hands of a Roman governor and his soldiers? Some readers have found Paul's image terrifying rather than endearing, provoking revulsion not love. Is it an image of child abuse or of generous self-giving love, of murder or life-giving love?

Cosmic Love

Paul also constructs God's love as world-changing. Literally. Nothing "in all creation will be able to separate us from the love of God in Christ Jesus our Lord," he asserts (Rom 8:39). He gets to this conclusion by way of six questions (in the NRSV translation). It reads like a courtroom scene at the final judgment. Human beings are on trial before God. But more than that, God's disposition toward people is on trial. How does God regard us? Is God turned toward us or turned away from us? Is God on our side? And Paul confidently, even triumphantly, makes the case that God's faithful love "for us" conquers all.

Paul's first question nails the issue. "If God is for us, who is against us?" (Rom 8:31). The initial "if" is not an expression of doubt; rather, we might translate it: "since it is so that God is for us . . . ." The assertion picks up all Paul has said about God in the previous chapters. This God is the creator (Rom 1:18-25), whose faithfulness cannot be overcome by human faithlessness (Rom 3:3), whose love reaches even to the depths of human torture in the form of crucifixion (Rom 5:6-10). Since this loving God is for us, is on our side, and embraces us in faithful love then nothing can resist God's love and those embraced in it.

With his second question, Paul again evokes Jesus's crucifixion as a display of God's love (Rom 8:32). Here the emphasis is on God's act of faithful self-giving—"he who did not withhold his own Son but gave him up for all of us." And this act guarantees God's loving faithfulness toward humans. It is the unchanging character of God that is on display in Jesus's death. (But—**Red-flag moment**—recall those questions about a parent consigning a child to such a death!)

In this context, Paul continues the courtroom rhetoric, daring anyone to bring a charge or accusation or issue a sentence of condemnation. To do so would be an exercise in futility. A charge against people is useless because God "justifies" or sets people in right relationship with God. A sentence of condemnation is impossible since God's loving power has raised Jesus from the dead to show that Roman power, sin, and death do not have the final word. God out-powers and out-loves them. Now Jesus joins forces with God to advocate for people.

Paul elaborates the impossibility of anybody or anything resisting God's love represented by Christ. He sets out a catalogue of seven hardships or vicissitudes that might pose a threat to God's love: "Who will separate us from the love of Christ? Will hardship, or distress, or persecution, or famine, or nakedness, or peril, or sword?" (Rom 8:35). All of these are external circumstances that Paul sees increasing in intensity toward the end of this present age dominated by all sorts of evil. *Hardship* and *distress* denote general difficult circumstances; *persecution* or prejudiced harassment is always a possibility from local communities who do not understand religious practices; *famine* and *nakedness* denote the lack of basic resources of food and clothing that was commonplace for poorer folks in the Roman Empire; and *peril* and the *sword* were constant threats in an empire that depended on military power and violence and did not care who became collateral damage.

Disastrous circumstances can readily be interpreted as signs of God's displeasure or punishment. Surely they are indications that God does not love us. Everybody who has tried to live in relation to God has had such thoughts.

But Paul's intent is to reframe these experiences. His point is that how people respond to or engage such situations depends on their perspectives. These situations might threaten or even destroy relationship with God—if one does not understand them in the context of the unsurpassed love of God that cannot be threatened or overcome by anything. Such experiences do not indicate that God has withdrawn or withheld God's love. Rather, God's powerful love is the very means by which these circumstances might be navigated. "No in all these things we are more than conquerors through him who loved us" (Rom 8:37).

If these circumstances are no problem for the experience of God's love, what's left? Paul's focus now broadens. He goes cosmic in time and space. Is there anything in all creation that can separate people from God's love? Pushing the language to the extremes, his answer is an emphatic no!

He frames his answer as a strongly worded assertion: "I am convinced." He traverses the cosmos with four contrasting pairs of cosmic realities and finds nothing to challenge God's love (Rom 8:38-39a). His first pair comprises "neither death nor life." Paul's assertion is that nothing in these fundamental parameters of human existence can separate people from God's love. Paul has already made this point by appealing to Jesus's death by crucifixion. Even there, there was no escape from God's love; in fact, it demonstrated the vastly inclusive, far-reaching, and all-embracing nature of God's love.

The next pair comprises "nor angels nor rulers." Just what is in view here is not entirely clear. *Angels* usually refers to heavenly beings, sometimes positive as agents of God and sometimes negative as opponents of God. Some angels are understood as heavenly patrons or "guardian angels" for particular nations. The term *rulers* could refer to angelic powers and demons, but it can also refer to earthly rulers. There was also an understanding that earthly rulers were particularly linked to and channeled heavenly powers or sponsors. Paul's language, then, is not specific and seems to be wide-ranging, embracing any and every heavenly and earthly power. His point? None of these powers, whether in heaven or on earth, can stop God's love embracing people.

The third pair stipulates periods of time: "neither things present nor things to come." Neither the present nor the new age on the horizon can interfere with God's loving. And the fourth pair, "nor height nor depth," stipulates the spatial axis of the cosmos. Nothing from the highest point of the heavens to the lowest depths of the earth or sea can thwart God's loving.

And in case Paul has not covered all his bases with his four pairings, he adds a cover-all phrase: "nor anything else in all creation" (Rom 8:39). The reference to creation recalls the discussion of God as the creator of the world in chapter 1. The creation belongs to the creator God and, Paul asserts, as sovereign of the cosmos, God's love embraces every aspect of it. Paul concludes triumphantly: nothing "in all creation will be able to separate us from the love of God in Christ Jesus our Lord" (Rom 8:39).

Paul's marvelous vision of God's all-embracing and triumphant love raises a couple of **Red-flag questions**. Here's the first. If God's love is so all-pervasive, how come parts of our planet and peoples on our planet often seem so unloved? It's one thing to assert that famines do not separate people from God's love, but it's hard to know why God's love does not prevent or overcome starvation, drought, or market/profit manipulation. A display of powerful love would supply the needed food! And likewise with the "sword" or the violence that wracks our planet. It's hard to see God's love in the midst of international strife, civil wars, and violent warlords. Of course, we can argue that humans create havoc and it's not God's responsibility—except Paul is adamant that God's love powerfully triumphs over all. Perhaps he is offering his readers a vision only of the future, the eschatological or end time triumph of God's love? But he does include "things present" as well as "things to come" in verse 38. How do we make sense of Paul's confident assertions in relation to daily experiences and realities on planet earth?

Here's the second question. Paul uses lots of "us" language in this passage. Who is the "us?" Who is embraced by such love? Just God's pets—the "elect" (Rom 8:33), some special group of "us" to whom most of "you" and "them" do not belong? How much love does God have to go around? How good do you have to be to join the exclusive club? To think further about these questions we need to turn to another passage in Romans.

What Does *All* Mean? (Rom 11:25-32)

Back in Romans chapter 3, Paul declared God's commitment to all people:

> Or is God the God of Jews only? Is he not the God of Gentiles also? Yes, of Gentiles also, since God is one; and he will justify the circumcised on the ground of faith and the uncircumcised through that same faith. (Rom 3:29-30).

That sounds fine, but Paul has a problem. He is well aware that Jewish folks were not responding to his proclamation in overwhelming numbers. So in chapters 9–11 he expresses his "great sorrow and unceasing anguish in my heart" about the rejection of his preaching by many Jewish folks (9:2) and then spends three chapters wrestling with what God is doing. In 11:25-32, he sets out his conclusions.

He does not back away from this confident assertion of God's purposes for all people—Jew and Gentile. Jewish folks have not been rejected by God. They remain "beloved" or embraced in God's love (Rom 11:28). But *how* is God-at-work? Paul sees several phases in God's program (he uses the word "mystery").

Phase 1: a "hardening" or partial and temporary resistance has come upon Israel (Rom 11:25).

Phase 2: during this time period (unspecified in length), Gentiles respond to God's grace.

Phase 3: "all Israel will be saved" (Rom 11:26).

There has been much debate as to how we should understand "all Israel." One possibility reads it as referring to the church. Another possibility reads it in reference to some Jewish folks (the elect). Neither of these possibilities is convincing. Paul has used "Israel" ten times in Romans 9–11 prior to 11:26, and all of them refer to literal or ethnic Israel. In this context, the reference here in 11:26 also refers to ethnic Israel. And the rest of 11:26-27 supports this interpretation as Paul cites a mixed-up version of (mostly) Isa 59:20-21, which declares God's faithfulness to the covenant with Israel. That is, Paul declares God will be faithful to ("righteous") God's commitments to Israel as well as to Gentiles. The future tense indicates God-at-work is not yet finished in accomplishing God's purposes.

Paul pulls all this together in a very succinct assertion about God-at-work: "For God has imprisoned all in disobedience so that he may be merciful to all" (Rom 11:32). God-at-work is not determined or defined by human actions or responses. Human sinfulness or faithlessness, whether Jew or Gentile, cannot thwart God's faithful accomplishment of God's purposes (Rom 3:3). So all humans are marked by disobedience, but God will "be merciful to all" and mercy all (yes, it's a verb) into relationship with God.

Inquiring minds of course want to know—how will God do this? Tell us, Paul. But in verses 33-36 Paul finishes the chapter with very different rhetoric. Explanation gives way to praise, clarification becomes mystery:

> O the depth of the riches and wisdom and knowledge of God! How unsearchable are his judgments and how inscrutable his ways. (Rom 11:33)

We might appreciate the sentiment, but it doesn't answer the questions! Perhaps the closest we might get is to recall that "mercy" is essentially a synonym for "love" and recognize that somehow, in the mysterious and inscrutable ways of God, God loves or woos people into relationship with God. As we know, love can do powerful things to us.

Does *All* Embrace Gender?

If *all* includes Jews and Gentiles, does it include women and men? Paul's discussion, like the scene with Cornelius in Acts 10–11 (discussed in chapter 9 above), has focused on ethnicity as Paul adamantly argues for God's love embracing all people while remaining faithful to Israel. But what about gender? Does Paul see God's love equally embracing male and female?

In the concluding chapter of Romans, chapter 16, Paul greets nearly thirty people in Rome. About a third of them are women. The language

Paul uses for these women recognizes them as leaders and coworkers with himself. They plant churches, preach, and teach as church leaders.

He begins by endorsing Phoebe, a leader in the church in Cenchreae near Corinth who may be carrying Paul's letter to Rome. He describes her first as a *deacon*, a word he uses elsewhere to describe his own preaching, church planting, and pastoring (1 Cor 3:5; 2 Cor 6:4). Then he calls her a *benefactor* or leader, again using a word he uses to describe is own actions (1 Thess 5:12). Phoebe does what Paul does.

Next, he greets a wife and husband pair, Prisca and Aquila, whom he describes as "working with me in Christ Jesus" (Rom 16:3-5), and he recognizes them as leaders of a house church (Rom 16:5; 1 Cor 16:19). Elsewhere he uses the noun "coworkers" to refer to his own identity as a coworker with God (1 Cor 3:9) and to refer to other male workers such as Titus (2 Cor 8:23), Epaphroditus (Phil 2:25-30), Philemon (Phlm 1:1), Urbanus, and Timothy (Rom 16:9, 21). To be a coworker is to be a preacher, church leader, and provider of pastoral care as Paul is. As a coworker, Prisca belongs in this company.

Paul greets four other women: Mary, Tryphaena, Tryphosa, and Persis (Rom 16:6, 12). He describes them as *working hard*, a verb that describes his own preaching and ministry (1 Cor 15:10-11; Gal 4:11; Phil 2:16), as well as other leaders in congregations (1 Cor 16:16; 1 Thess 5:12). In Romans 16:7, he refers to another woman, Junia, whom he identifies as being "prominent among the apostles." The identification of a woman as an apostle was too much for some male interpreters across the church's history, so they made her into a man! But Junia is a woman's name, and the woman Junia is among the church leaders, planters, and teachers.

In this passage, then, Paul's *all* recognizes that God's love embraces both Jews and Gentiles, women and men.

Questions for Reflection/Discussion

1. If God's love is all-pervasive as Paul claims in Romans 8:35-39, how come parts of our planet and peoples on our planet often seem as though they do not experience God's love? How do we account for both Paul's claim and our daily realities?

2. What do you think of Paul's claim in Romans 5:6-10 that God's giving his son to die on a Roman cross is an act of love? Look at how Paul makes a somewhat similar argument in 1 Corinthians 1:18–2:16, where Paul emphasizes the display of God's foolishness and weakness.

3. How might these texts help us understand and locate ourselves in the debate over inclusiveness that is happening across Christian communities (involving women, LGBTQ, race, nationality, refugees, and immigrants)?

Further Reading

Warren Carter and Amy-Jill Levine, *The New Testament: Methods and Meanings* (Nashville: Abingdon, 2013), 112–28.

Chapter 13

The Household of God and Its Male Guardians (1 Tim 3:1-15; 2 Tim 2:14-26)

> *Read 1 Timothy 3:1-15; 2 Timothy 2:14-26 before reading the chapter. Then refer to them while you read the chapter.*

The writer of 1 and 2 Timothy has a lot to say about God. Most of it occurs in either creedal, confessional, or doxological (praise) statements, or in statements that sanction moral actions. Here's a sample:

- To the King of the ages, immortal, invisible, the only God, be honor and glory forever and ever. Amen. (1 Tim 1:17)

- Pray for kings and all who are in high positions, so that we may lead a quiet and peaceable life in all godliness and dignity. This is right and is acceptable in the sight of God our Savior, who desires everyone to be saved and to come to the knowledge of the truth. For there is one God; there is also one mediator between God and humankind, Christ Jesus. (1 Tim 2:2-5)

- For everything created by God is good, and nothing is to be rejected, provided it is received with thanksgiving. (1 Tim 4:4)

- For to this end we toil and struggle, because we have our hope set on the living God, who is the Savior of all people, especially of those who believe. (1 Tim 4:10)

- In the presence of God, who gives life to all things, and of Christ Jesus, who in his testimony before Ponius Pilate made the good confession (1 Tim 6:13)

- which [God] will bring about at the right time—he who is the blessed and only Sovereign, the King of kings and Lord of lords. It is he alone who has immortality and dwells in unapproachable light, whom no one has ever seen or can see; to him be honor and eternal dominion. Amen. (1 Tim 6:15-16)

- As for those who in the present age are rich, command them not to be haughty, or to set their hopes on the uncertainty of riches, but rather on God who richly provides us with everything for our enjoyment. (1 Tim 6:17)

- For this reason I remind you to rekindle the gift of God that is within you through the laying on of my hands; for God did not give us a spirit of cowardice, but rather a spirit of power and of love and of self-discipline. (2 Tim 1:6-7)

- But the word of God is not chained. (2 Tim 2:9)

- But the Lord stood by me and gave me strength, so that through me the message might be fully proclaimed and all the Gentiles might hear it. So I was rescued from the lion's mouth. The Lord will rescue me from every evil attack and save me for his heavenly kingdom. To him be the glory forever and ever. Amen. (2 Tim 4:17-18)

Who Is the Author of 1 and 2 Timothy?

Both 1 and 2 Timothy claim in their opening verses that Paul is their author. Most interpreters, though, think this is unlikely and that disciples of Paul who lived a generation or two after Paul's death wrote the letters. Writing in the name of a venerated teacher was a common and honorable practice in the ancient world. The use of

Paul's name does not identify the author but lends authority and prestige to the letters. How do interpreters make this decision?

1. Already in the second century, church figures such as Marcion, Tatian, and the manuscript known as p46 did not include these letters among those written by Paul.

2. Scholars note that about one-third of their 900 words do not appear elsewhere in Paul, 175 of them are not used elsewhere in the NT, and about 200 are common in second-century Christian writings.

3. The style of writing also differs from Paul's with longer, well connected sentences and without the questions and answers and anticipated objections of Paul's diatribe style (e.g., Rom 3:29-30; 6:1-2a).

4. It is difficult to fit these letters into what is known about Paul's life and activities from the rest of Paul's letters or from Acts.

5. In Paul's letters, he argues with his opponents. In these letters, the writer advocates ignoring opponents (2 Tim 2:23-24).

6. While Paul recognizes a charismatic structure in his churches (Rom 12; 1 Cor 12–14), the writer of these letters has a hierarchy of male leaders called elders, bishops, and deacons (1 Tim 3).

7. These letters have different theological emphases. The cross hardly gets a mention; the return of Jesus, though mentioned, has little significance; the "body of Christ" is not used; the term *faith* does not designate a dynamic relationship of trust but refers to "the faith," a body of doctrine.

8. While Paul recognizes women as coworkers (Rom 16), these letters restrict women to child bearing (1 Tim 2:11-15) and prohibit women leaders of church groups.

Some important emphases recur through these verses. One strand highlights God's greatness and otherness or transcendence. So God is the only or one God. God is the ruler or king or Lord. God is immortal, invisible, and worthy of praise. Yet a second strand highlights God-at-work among people. As Savior, God desires to save all. The living God is the creator and provides all good things for people. God is powerful and empowers people to serve God. The loving God is present and active among people.

As important as these images are, 1 and 2 Timothy present another image for God, one that draws together several passages in the letters. The writer constructs God as a house owner. The writer tells Timothy—whom he identifies subsequently as a "man of God," thereby linking him with Moses (Deut 33:1), Samuel (1 Sam 9:6, 10), and a prophet (1 Kgs 13:1)—that he writes the letter so that:

> You may know how one ought to behave in the household of God which is the church of the living God, the pillar and bulwark of the truth. (1 Tim 3:15)

The Greek word translated here as "household" could be translated simply as "house." We will engage both dimensions in the discussion below.

This image of God's house evokes several biblical traditions. Throughout its long history, the temple in Jerusalem was known as God's house. God rebukes David through the prophet Nathan for not building a house for God (2 Sam 7:1-7), and Solomon builds the temple/house for God (1 Kgs 6:11-14). The house of God is a place where God was understood to dwell:

> O LORD, I love the house in which you dwell and the place where your glory abides. (Ps 26:8)

Because of God's presence, it becomes a place of security and peace in which people dwell (Ps 23:6), to which people gather together to encounter God (Pss 55:14; 65:3-4):

> My tears have been my food both day and night, while people say to me continually, "Where's your God now?" These things I remember as I pour out my soul: how I went with the throng, and led them in procession to the house of God, with glad shouts and songs of thanksgiving, a multitude keeping festival. (Ps 42:3-4)

The Household of God and Its Male Guardians (1 Tim 3:1-15; 2 Tim 2:14-26)

It was the place in which people gathered to worship God:

> Happy are those who live in your house, ever singing your praise. (Ps 84:4)

> I was pleased when they said to me, "Let us go to the house of the LORD." (Ps 122:1)

Several prophets, though, protested ways in which God's house became something of a gigantic lucky penny for some people. The prophet Jeremiah complains about those who practice social injustice by exploiting the most vulnerable members of society (the alien/immigrant, orphan, and widow) in defiance of God's will, yet presumed to believe that the presence of God's house would keep the people safe from divine punishment (Jer 7). Jeremiah declares that the temple is not a lucky charm. Jeremiah's God demands that worship and social justice must accompany each other.

The prophet Ezekiel exposes another abuse of God's house. He witnesses violations of "the house of the Lord" such as images, idols, and worship of the sun god (Ezek 8). These practices disobeyed the first two of the Ten Commandments against having gods other than God, and making idols and images (Exod 20:2-6). As with Jeremiah, Ezekiel links false worship in God's house with social injustice throughout the land, notably increased violence (Ezek 8:17).

The house of God, the temple in Jerusalem, was burned to the ground when the Romans captured Jerusalem in 70 CE. Several decades after this event when there was no temple in Jerusalem, the writer of 1 Timothy coopts the tradition of "God's house" and now uses the phrase to designate not the Jerusalem temple but the community of Jesus-believers as God's house/hold (1 Tim 3:15).

By borrowing the phrase, the writer makes some big claims about this community in relation to God. By calling it the house/hold of God, the writer asserts it to be the place of God's dwelling and presence. It is the living God who owns this house, a place of gathering together of people who encounter God in worship. This community gathered in God's presence is, to continue the temple metaphor, the "pillar and foundation of the truth." In the letter, *truth* seems to denote knowing or understanding the faith, a body of doctrine about God and Jesus. The reference to "pillar and foundation" suggests that this divinely inhabited house is stable and solid.

Leaders, Overseers, Guardians

Just as the "house/temple of God" in Jerusalem had human leadership or overseers, so too does 1 Timothy's "house/hold of God." In the Jerusalem temple/house of God, the leadership comprised priests with the chief priests functioning not just as religious leaders but also as sociopolitical leaders who ruled in alliance with the Roman governors like Pilate. 1 Timothy's leaders are not priests nor societal leaders, but they comprise two groups of men who are to be leaders in the communities of Jesus-followers.

The first group comprises bishops (1 Tim 3:1-7). The word translated "bishop" literally means an "overseer." In the ancient world, it referred to people in positions of oversight, often involving financial matters, but also exercising leadership in civic and religious organizations. The writer spells out a job description for bishops comprising at least eighteen characteristics (depending on how you count them). Most of them are moral qualities; there's a predictable, functional skill of being "an apt teacher" (1 Tim 3:2) but no reference to any liturgical leadership. There is, though, one quality that stands out:

> He must manage his own household well, keeping his children submissive and respectful in every way—for if someone does not know how to manage his own household, how can they take care of God's church? (1 Tim 3:4-5)

This emphasis on household management is also reflected in the requirement that the bishop or overseer be "married only once." The writer makes a clear connection between management of one's own house and management of God's house. If you can't keep your own house in order, you aren't fit to be an overseer of God's house.

Despite the use of the male pronoun *he* throughout, the English translation plays down a crucial qualification for a bishop or overseer of "God's church." He must be a man. The literal translation of 3:2 ("married only once") reads "husband of one wife." According to the writer, leadership

The Household of God and Its Male Guardians (1 Tim 3:1-15; 2 Tim 2:14-26)

of God's house/hold is not a role for women or for the divorced or for the never-married. The writer's God apparently favors men over women for this leadership role. This is quite different from Paul's affirmation of partnership with women in Romans 16.[1] The **Red flag** is waving.

How might we understand this gender preference in 1 and 2 Timothy?

One factor, of course, is that both letters are addressed to a man, Timothy. But beyond this is another important factor. There was a philosophical tradition in the ancient world concerned with "household management." From Aristotle through to first- and second-century writers such as Philodemus, Hierocles, and Jews such as Philo and Josephus, this tradition argued that an ideal (elite) household comprised four dynamics. The ideal household was centered on the male as head of the household. This male had three roles: husband who ruled over his wife, father who ruled over his children, and master who ruled over his slaves. The verb *ruled over* emphasizes his dominance and authority. In addition, this leading male represented the household in public and was responsible for financial and property management.

We can't imagine that every household in the ancient world was so organized. It wasn't. This ideal pattern did not shape most people's household experiences. But nevertheless, this "ideal" did express a dominant cultural value of male dominance or patriarchy that pervaded not only households but society in general. The writer of 1 Timothy imitates this cultural pattern. The **Red flag** is waving. He takes it over and adopts it for the house/hold of God. He makes the house/hold of God into a religious copy of this ideal, male-dominated cultural pattern. In doing so, he constructs God as one who sanctions this form of male governance for the household or church of God. First Timothy's God conforms to and secures, but does not challenge, this cultural pattern of male dominance.

In addition to this male overseer who, like the husband-father-master of the ideal household, is "well thought of by outsiders" (1 Tim 3:7), deacons or "servers" have some sort of role in the house/hold of God. Again, the job description of verses 8-13 is long on moral qualities and very thin on duties. Again their ability to control their own households is emphasized (3:12).

There is, though, one significant addition. Deacons or servers are not only males; women can be deacons (1 Tim 3:11). But what are they to do? Elsewhere, the term refers to Phoebe in Romans 16:1 who is a church leader and benefactor. Given the presence of male bishops or overseers in this chapter, it is unlikely that women were leaders of the whole congregation.

In fact, in chapter 5, the writer is very concerned with the behavior and roles of widows in the house of God. He says widows are to devote themselves to their families and to prayer (1 Tim 5:1-8). The writer is very suspicious of younger widows and not at all complimentary about them (5:9-16). They are, according to the writer, so obsessed with getting married that they lose their faith, they become idle and gossips and busybodies! The writer wants them to have babies and take care of their own households (5:13-14). With all this male stereotyping of women (the **Red flag** is still waving), the writer exhibits male biases and copies male-sanctioned cultural patterns of controlling women by domesticating them and confining them to particular household roles. But unlike his presentation of bishops or overseers, he does not here appeal to God to sanction his prejudices.

God's Approved Worker

In 2 Timothy 2:14-26, the writer continues to elaborate the qualities of "Timothy" as a male worker in the house of God approved by God (2:15). Throughout, the writer references God's presence and returns to the image of the house/hold. What sort of approved representative of God is Timothy to be?

Verse 15 reminds Timothy of his central motivation to be approved by God:

> Do your best to present yourself to God as one approved by him, a worker who has no need to be ashamed, rightly explaining the word of truth. (2 Tim 2:15)

First Timothy 2:14-18 elaborate one dimension of this approval, namely the ability to use words to explain "the word of truth." Timothy is to represent God faithfully and accurately in proclaiming the gospel mes-

The Household of God and Its Male Guardians (1 Tim 3:1-15; 2 Tim 2:14-26)

sage about God and Jesus. This task is set in a difficult context of conflict in which Timothy's appropriate talk is to contrast with destructive talk. There is "wrangling," "profane chatter," "talk [that spreads] like gangrene," and false proclamation about the resurrection having already taken place that is "upsetting the faith of some." The writer even names two of the people he regards as opponents (Hymenaeus and Philetus; 2 Tim 2:14, 16-18). The image of a spreading disease, gangrene, underlines the destructive effect of such inappropriate talk. So the writer evokes God the (scary) judge in instructing Timothy to "warn them before God" (1 Tim 2:14). Appropriate talk is an important quality for the worker in God's house who presents himself to God as approved (1 Tim 2:15).

The writer then returns to the house/hold metaphor, notably its "firm foundation," to make two affirmations about the God whose approval is sought. On the solid and reliable foundation of the house/hold of God that cannot be shaken by any opponents and their false words are two inscriptions. Both inscriptions say something about God and something about being a member of God's house. The first declares God's close and intimate relationship with "those who are his" (2 Tim 2:19). God establishes this house/hold and its foundation in this intimate bond of God's knowledge of each member.

The second inscription asserts God's demand in this relationship. Each member is required to "turn away from wickedness." God demands from each person a moral response, a life of ongoing conversion from evil. God demands moral accountability.

The writer develops God's demand for moral accountability by moving from the foundation of the house/hold of God to inside the house and to its utensils (2 Tim 2:20-21). The utensils are a metaphor for the people in God's house/hold. Verse 20 runs the gamut of gold to clay utensils, from special to ordinary vessels. Verse 21 makes the identifications. Those who "turn away from wickedness," who purify their moral attitudes and relational practices, are "special utensils, dedicated and useful to the owner of the house, ready for every good work" (1 Tim 2:21). Presumably those who do not engage this process of cleansing are "ordinary" utensils. But nothing further is said about them. There is no declaration, for example, that God cleans house and throws them out of God's house/hold!

Verses 22-26 elaborate the cleansing process with a movement between things to avoid/shun and things to embrace. So on one hand "shun youthful passions" but on the other, "pursue righteousness, faith, love, and peace" (2 Tim 2:22). Avoid "senseless controversies . . . quarrels" but be "kindly to everyone, an apt teacher, patient, correcting opponents with gentleness" (2:24-25). Such pastoral work might result in God's active intervention that causes some to "repent and come to know the truth" (2:25). Keeping peace within the house of God is an important task for the worker in God's house who presents himself to God as approved (2:25).

Recall the quote from Jeremiah 7 earlier in the chapter where the prophet links worship in God's house with the practice of social justice in society. By contrast, here in 2 Timothy, membership in God's house is linked with personal morality and relationships within the household.

In these verses, Timothy is called God's "slave" or "servant" in God's house (2 Tim 2:24). The term continues the house-of-God image by evoking the terribly dehumanizing institution of slavery. Here (**Red-flag alert**) the institution is reinscribed and used without any hesitation or critique. God is constructed not only as a house owner but also as a slave owner. To be a slave was to live only for the master's pleasure and to execute the master's will. To be a slave of an exalted master was to gain some honor, so to be a slave of the creator and savior of the world was a means by which a slave might gain some prestige by association. Nevertheless, slavery's terrible history of dehumanizing human lives and bodies cautions us about its use to construct images of God and of human-divine interaction.

Questions for Reflection/Discussion

1. Select some of the passages from 1 and 2 Timothy quoted in the opening pages of this chapter. Look at the passages in context in the letter. What does each one say about God and how does it function in the letter? Is God the object of praise or used to provide authority for instruction or exhortation or . . . ?

2. Sum up the letter's construction of God as a house owner. What does this construction say about God and about God's house and personnel in it?

3. The discussion above has emphasized that being a man was a crucial requirement for leadership in the house of God according to the writer of these letters. Review those passages, along with the passages severely limiting the roles of women (1 Tim 2:8-15; 3:1-13; 5:3-16). Why does the writer have such a problem with women leaders and insist on male leaders? What does this emphasis say about God in the presentation of 1 and 2 Timothy? Recall Paul's partnership with women in Romans 16 (discussed at the end of ch. 12 above).

4. A textbox near the beginning of this chapter suggests 1 and 2 Timothy were not actually written by Paul despite what their opening verses say. What do you think of this matter and the eight factors identified in the textbox? Does the likelihood that Paul did not write these letters bother you? Do you understand this possibility as a challenge to the authority of the text itself? Why? Why not?

Further Reading

Warren Carter and Amy-Jill Levine, *The New Testament: Methods and Meanings* (Nashville: Abingdon, 2013), 238–54.

Joseph Fitzmyer, "The Savior God: The Pastoral Epistles," in *The Forgotten God: Perspectives in Biblical Theology,* ed. Andrew Das and Frank Matera (Louisville: Westminster, 2002), 181–96.

Deborah Krause, *1 Timothy* (London: T&T Clark, 2004).

Elsa Tamez, *Struggles for Power in Early Christianity: A Study of the First Letter to Timothy* (Maryknoll, NY: Orbis, 2007).

Chapter 14

God the Friend
(Jas 4:1–5:6)

> *Read James 4:1-5:6 before reading the chapter. Then refer to them while you read the chapter.*

On my first day in the United States, I left the hotel to find some affordable food for my young family. I stepped off the sidewalk to cross the road. Suddenly there was a screeching of tires, a blaring of horns, and a taxi going sideways slid past me. The taxi came to a halt and a very red-faced taxi-driver emerged, and with much waving of arms and gesturing with fingers, he launched into a loud and long monologue. His starting point was a touching concern as to whether my eyes were working properly or whether my eyesight, even with my glasses, might be impaired. He then wondered if I was deficient in common sense and intelligence. Developing the point but apparently seeking dialogue, he asked me if I was too &¢$%#@ing dumb to live. Before I could respond, he redirected his rhetoric to my character. He asked if I was so self-centered, so self-absorbed, so oblivious to other people that I did not care if my selfishness resulted in the deaths of others. I must admit I didn't see anybody dead, but his point was clear. Then, again without giving me a chance to reply, changing direction and now getting nasty, he inquired about the legitimacy of my birth and—and this piece really hurt—he raised some concerns about my mother's morals in conceiving me. To cap it all off, he suggested it may well have been better if I had been put down at birth so that I would not endanger the wellbeing of other law-abiding citizens. Then with a gesture that was readily understandable cross-culturally, he drove off.

I had heard the United States could be welcoming or hostile to foreigners so I put it down to the latter option. A little later, having procured some food, I returned to the hotel. As I was about to cross the road, I suddenly realized why the taxi-driver had been upset with me. For thirty years of my life, when I crossed the road in my home country, I looked to the right to see if any traffic was approaching. But now, it dawned on me, in this country with cars driving on the "other" side of the road, I should look to the left, not the right! By not looking to the left, I had nearly gotten myself killed and had scared the daylights out of the poor taxi-driver who had just managed to evade me. I think that's what he was telling me—in his own graphic way. I realized that if I was going to survive in this country, I needed to learn better ways of fitting in with local customs!

The early Jesus movement had to work out how it would make its way in its cultural context of the Roman Empire. We saw one example of this in the last chapter on 1 and 2 Timothy. I pointed out that the writer of 1 and 2 Timothy focuses on fitting in and accommodating to his society. To be *at home* in his society, he borrows a dominant societal structure—the household—to construct God as a house owner. He imitates philosophical discussions and societal practices in reinscribing male-centered or patriarchal control of the house/hold of God. The Roman emperor was understood to be the "father of the fatherland," the head of a great household over which he ruled. Imitating a male-dominated society, the writer insists the bishop be a well-respected male in the wider society. There's little room for women's leadership.

In the letter of James (which is probably not written by James the brother of Jesus), we see a quite different approach to negotiating the larger society. This document is not interested in fitting in to the larger society of the Roman Empire dominated by a small powerful and wealthy elite presiding over a hierarchical and patriarchal society. James's priority is to delineate where God-at-work might be found. Commitment to this

God the Friend (Jas 4:1–5:6)

God ought to put Jesus-followers at odds with the values, practices, and structures of the ruling elite.

This desired antipathy is expressed through the document's construction of being a friend of God in contrast to "friendship with the world." The writer of James equates "friendship with the world" with hostility to or "enmity with God." But the writer recognizes that "friendship with the world" exists among those who want to be or who see themselves as "friends" with God:

> Adulterers! Do you not know that friendship with the world is enmity with God? Therefore whoever wishes to be a friend of the world becomes an enemy of God. (Jas 4:4)

The intensity with which the writer understands this antithesis between "the world" and God is expressed in the writer's offensive description of his audience as "adulterers." This is an image of disloyalty or faithlessness, not a literal statement about illicit sexual activity. The metaphor of illicit sexual activity was commonly used in the Hebrew scriptures to condemn Israel for being unfaithful to their covenant "marriage" with God by their involvement with the nations and susceptibility to idolatry (Jer 3:6-10). Using a related though different sexual image for covenant unfaithfulness, Psalm 106 expresses the idea:

> But they mingled with the nations and learned to do as they did. They served their idols which became a snare to them. . . . They sacrificed to the idols of Canaan; and the land was polluted with blood. Thus they became unclean by their acts, and prostituted themselves in their doings. (Ps 106:35-39)

What has the audience of James done to merit such a harsh condemnation as "adulterers"? What has their "friendship with the world" looked like that arouses the writer's hostility and God's enmity and prevents them being friends with God? It's hard to know for sure (the writer does not attack idols) though James 4:1-3 lists some behaviors of which the writer disapproves: fighting among themselves, out of control passions and coveting, misguided desires that result in inappropriate prayers. And—**Red-flag alert**—the writer seems to blame the poor for their own poverty.

Their selfish and indulgent desires, not oppressive socioeconomic systems, explain why "you do not have because you do not ask" (4:3).

We get some further clues from two of the writer's previous uses of the term *world* earlier in the document—each in antithesis to God. The first use of *world* occurs in a context that emphasizes moral behavior and actions of social justice that the world does not practice. The writer condemns "worthless" religion in which a person runs off at the mouth and cannot control their speech. By contrast,

> religion that is pure and undefiled before God the Father, is this: to care for orphans and widows in their distress, and to keep oneself unstained by the world. (Jas 1:27)

God-at-work with fatherly care is expressed in actions that are outlined across the scripture, namely care for orphans and widows (Exod 22:21-24; Isa 1:10-17). To be "unstained by the world" is to live according to God's will that particularly attends to the needy, the weak, and the vulnerable, something that "the world" does not do. To be friends with the world is to embody its values and practices of selfish and indulgent desires and practices that preserve the elite-benefitting status quo and continues the neglect of the vulnerable. This critique indicates that "the world" comprises elite control and practices in the Roman Empire.

The second use of *world* continues to underscore the antithesis between these self-benefitting practices and God's purposes. In the next section (Jas 2:1-7), the writer protests those in his audience who commit "acts of favoritism" for the rich while ignoring or "dishonoring" the poor. This critique draws on a lengthy theme throughout the Hebrew scriptures in which God especially attends to the vulnerable and the poor and against the powerful rich who exploit them (Isa 3:14-15; 10:1-3; Ezek 16:49; Amos 4:1; 8:4-6). Actions, or in the letter's language, "works" such as flattering the rich, showing favoritism to the rich, and despising and oppressing the poor replicate the world's or Roman Empire's values and structures that destroy human interactions. Not only does this behavior leave the oppressive actions of the rich unchecked, it violates God-at-work in favoring the poor:

> Has not God chosen the poor in the world to be rich in faith and to be heirs of the kingdom that he has promised to those who love him? But you have dishonored the poor. Is it not the rich who oppress you? Is it not they who drag you into court? (Jas 2:5-6)

While the writer constructs God's favoritism for the poor positively, he calls favoritism for the rich "blasphemy" (Jas 2:7).

The next section in chapter 2 elaborates friendship with God as doing God's will (Jas 2:8-10). That is, while God has favoritism for the poor and not the rich, the writer does not construct God as actively, arbitrarily, and directly changing this basic structure of the Roman world as Luke 1:52-54 does (see the discussion in ch. 6 above). Rather, the writer places a premium on human agents and action in accord with divine wishes. He appeals to the "royal law," the law God revealed through Moses, as the divine will to be obeyed. Particularly, countering favoritism to the rich, he quotes Leviticus 19:18b:

> You do well if you really fulfill the royal law according to the scripture, "You shall love your neighbor as yourself." But if you show partiality, you commit sin and are convicted by the law as transgressors. For whoever keeps the whole law but fails in one point has become accountable for all of it. (Jas 2:8-10)

Here the reference to "your neighbor" in the quotation from Leviticus 19:18b refers to the poor. And "love" is understood to require practical actions or works:

> What good is it, my brothers and sisters, if you say you have faith but do not have works? Can faith save you? If a brother or sister is naked and lacks daily food and one of you says to them, "Go in peace; keep warm and eat your fill," and yet you do not supply their bodily needs, what is the good of that? So faith by itself, if it has no works, is dead. (Jas 2:14-17)

To not be a friend of the world, to not be at enmity with God, to have God as one's friend requires a way of life that engages those who are casualties of the injustices caused by the rich in their contemporary imperial society ("the world"; Jas 2:6). The writer cites the example of Abraham, who obeyed God in doing his God-directed work. The obedient Abraham, is called "the friend of God" (Jas 2:21-23).

The "world," then, refers to the writer's contemporary society, notably the Roman Empire with its hierarchical structure that benefitted the wealthy, powerful, and high-status ruling elites to the disadvantage of the poor who lacked options and resources. To be friends with the "world" is to share and defend the elite empire's commitments. It is to value their ways and structures of envy, selfish ambition, self-aggrandizing competition, conflict, and pleasure (Jas 3:13-4:2). The writer claims that God is opposed to such structures and practices, which of course continue in our world, and claims that God subversively favors instead the wellbeing of the poor. To be friends of God is to share God's commitments and to live actively with works that are in solidarity with and that sustain the vulnerable against the powerful elite (Jas 4:4).

But the writer recognizes this is difficult because "the world" is all-pervasive, even among Jesus-followers. The church is not insulated against such values and practices. "God yearns jealously for the spirit that he has made to dwell in us" (Jas 4:5). This is a notoriously difficult verse to understand. There are several difficulties. The verse claims to quote the scriptures, but no one has found the scriptural origin of the verse! And while the NRSV translation says that God yearns jealously, the Greek text does not refer to God. And how are we to understand the term *spirit*—is it the human spirit of life or the Holy Spirit or something else? There is no room here to discuss all the difficulties, so I am going to assume that the verse continues the antithesis between friendship with the world or with God.

In this context, the writer says that God has made a spirit "to dwell in us" that, it seems, ought to help people live as friends of God. Regrettably, however, people (apparently influenced by the devil; Jas 4:7) have chosen "friendship with the world" instead. How does God respond? Not by giving up but by "giving all the more grace" to people to empower them to live appropriately as friends of God (Jas 4:6). The power of this greater grace or favor exemplifies God-at-work in generous and ungrudging giving (Jas 1:5) whereby "every generous act of giving . . . is from above, coming down from the Father of lights" and that is at work among God's creatures (Jas 1:17-18).

Four times in the next four verses, the writer refers to this God with whom his audience is to be friends (Jas 4:6-10). The passage is dominated by imperatives that spell out a process of renouncing friendship with the world and being friends with God. First, the writer announces God-at-work in the imperial world through "opposing the proud but giving grace to the humble" (Jas 4:6). The proud or arrogant refers to those who dominate and define "the world" as a structure and practices that oppose God. They comprise the elite marked by power, wealth, and status who oppress the poor and drag them into court (Jas 2:6). The grace given to the humble, then, embraces those committed to rejecting friendship with the world and embracing friendship with God. The humble are empowered to do the works that engage the vulnerable and needy.

The second reference to God moves from an announcement about God-at-work to a demand for human action (Jas 4:7). The command, "submit yourselves therefore to God," begins a process that effects a change of orientation and lifestyle to one based in God as God's friends. The writer addresses those among his audience whom he designates friends with the world, adulterers (Jas 4:4), and the proud or arrogant (Jas 4:6). To submit to God involves resisting the devil. The reference to the devil identifies the cosmic force opposed to God and at work in making friends with the world. Its power, though, is susceptible to resistance that causes the devil to flee (Jas 4:7).

The third reference elaborates the process of submitting to God. Having resisted the devil, drawing near to or approaching God is the next step (Jas 4:8). God is constructed as available and approachable, reciprocating the initiative of people who approach God (Jas 4:8). People, though, must approach God with purity of hands (designating actions or how one lives) and purity of heart (designating one's central commitments) in accord with God's purposes.

The writer underscores the need for their response by calling them "double-minded," wanting to be friends with both the world and God. Back in Jas 1:7, the "doubleminded" are described as "doubters" and "unstable." By using this designation, the writer reveals his effort to draw a line in the sand, to create an either-or identity that removes ambiguity and clearly demarcates those committed to God and not to the world. The conversion process requires their lamenting, mourning, and weeping over their double-mindedness. Their current laughter and joy, reflecting their friendship with the world, has to be reversed by mourning and dejection.

The fourth reference sums up the conversion process. Its key activity is humbling before God (Jas 4:10). The verb of humbling means becoming lowly economically and thereby joining a group who enjoy God's favor. God humbles or makes low the proud and arrogant but exalts those of humble status:

> The haughtiness of people shall be humbled and the pride of everyone shall be brought low; and the LORD alone will be exalted on that day. (Isa 2:17; also Ps 18:27)

> Let the believer who is lowly boast in being raised up, and the rich in being brought low because the rich will disappear like a flower in the field. (Jas 1:9-10)

Three Examples

Then in James 4:11–5:6, the writer offers three instances of the behaviors of those who are friends with the world (4:4), the arrogant and proud (4:6) who must heed the call to submit to God. The scenes' behaviors involve judging (4:11-12), arrogant self-assertion (4:13-17), and exploitation by the greedy rich (5:1-6). Each scene seeks to expose and change the behavior. And each scene constructs a different image of God that functions to counter and correct the behavior.

In the first of the three examples, the unacceptable behavior involves speaking evil about and judging others (Jas 5:11). In hierarchical, imperial society, as in our world, where status was displayed with fine adornment, clothes, and public honoring (Jas 2:2-4), public evaluation, competition, loss of honor, and social condemnation were commonplace. These same practices and mind-sets were, not surprisingly, practiced among Jesus-followers ("brothers and sisters") in speaking evil or slander. The writer declares that slander judges not only a person but also the law because by neglecting the law, the person puts himself or herself above the law of loving one's neighbor (Jas 2:8, evoking Lev 19:18). In doing so, the person plays the role of God in determining or judging what part of the law to obey or not. The selectivity thereby means they create their own law and God becomes obsolete. They dishonor the others about whom they speak evil.

The problem, says the writer, is that "there is one lawgiver and judge who is able to save and to destroy" (Jas 4:12). God, the one lawgiver and judge, has given a law requiring love for a neighbor rather than speaking evil against them and judging them. The writer constructs God as able to "save" or to "destroy," thereby providing an incentive and warning for his audience to change their ways of social interaction. To do so is to renounce friendship with the world and become friends with God.

The second scene involves arrogant self-assertion in which people—those with some resources for business and money-making—plan their lives without reference to God. They presume to live as though they are masters of their own lives. In contrast to such arrogance, the writer constructs God as sovereign, and God's will should be the determinative point of reference for daily life:

> Instead you ought to say: "If the Lord wishes, we will live and do this or that." (Jas 4:15)

To not live in this way is to sin against God.

The third scene escalates the rhetoric in a sharp denunciation of the rich elite (Jas 5:1-6). Their hoardings of riches, fine clothing, gold, and silver are depicted in ruins and decay that represent God's judgment (5:2-3). Then follows a catalogue of practices whereby they have enhanced their wealth by oppressing the poor. They have defrauded agricultural laborers and harvesters by withholding their wages. They have thereby sustained a life of self-indulgence, extravagance, luxury, and pleasure. They have fattened their hearts for "a day of slaughter" (5:5). They "have condemned and murdered the righteous one, who does not resist you" (5:6). The reference to murder might reflect explicit attacks on rivals or it might indicate the effects of their exploitative actions in starving the poor to death.

The writer sets their oppressive actions and the protests of the exploited poor in relation to "the Lord of hosts" who has heard the cries of the exploited harvesters (Jas 5:4). The language of God hearing people's cries echoes biblical scenes of God's people crying out in Egyptian slavery (Exod 3:7) or the cries of mistreated widows, orphans, and the poor (Exod 22:21-27). God is understood to respond to such cries with restorative actions. The construction of God as "the Lord of hosts" underlines this aggressive divine responsiveness (Jas 5:4). This image of God-at-work particularly expresses God's power in creation (Ps 89:5-14) and in actions against the exploitative rich (Isa 5:7-16). It also constructs God as a warrior who supports Israel's armies:

> But David said to the Philistine, "You come to me with sword and spear and javelin, but I come to you in the name of the LORD of hosts, the God of the armies of Israel, whom you have defied. This very day the LORD will deliver you into my hand, and I will strike you down and cut off your head; and I will give the dead bodies of the Philistine army this very day to the birds of the air and to the wild animals of the earth so that all the earth may know that there is a God in Israel. (1 Sam 17:45-46)

The construction of God as "the Lord of hosts"—**Red-flag alert**—emphasizes God's militaristic power but in the service of justice. Here the writer sets this image of God over against the rich and promises that this all-powerful God will wage retributive war against the rich on behalf of the exploited laborers and harvesters. Why, then—further **Red-flag alert**—do the rich prosper and the poor get poorer?

This passage (Jas 4:1–5:6) constructs a range of images of God. Throughout is implied, but never mentioned, the image of God as friend, the God with whom the writer's audience can be friends if they abandon friendship with the world and submit to and draw near to God with purity and single-mindedness. God-at-work graces the poor to enable them to become friends and opposes the arrogant rich. Yet—**Red flag**—this God is also lawgiver and judge for those who resist this grace and refuse to live in reverence to God. The rich are especially vulnerable. The powerful warrior-God, responsive to the cries of the exploited poor, will act on their behalf against the oppressive rich.

God the Friend (Jas 4:1–5:6)

Questions for Reflection/Discussion

1. What does God's favor for the poor look like? Consider James 1:9-11; 1:27–2:7; 5:1-6, and Hebrew Bible passages such as Exodus 22:21-27; Isa 3:14-15; 5:7-17; 10:1-3; Ezekiel 16:49; Amos 4:1; 8:4-6.

2. If we are among the rich, how do we respond to passages like James 1:9-11; 2:1-7; and 5:1-6?

3. What is "friendship with the world"? Why and how does it impair friendship with God? What issues about engaging culture does this construction raise for contemporary communities of faith?

Further Reading

Luke Johnson, "Friendship with the World/Friendship with God," in *Discipleship in the New Testament*, ed. F. Segovia (Philadelphia: Fortress, 1985), 166–83.

Elsa Tamez, *The Scandalous Message of James* (New York: Crossroad, 1992).

Chapter 15

All You Need Is Love? (1 John 3–4)

> *Read 1 John 3–4 before reading this chapter. Then refer to them while you read the chapter.*

As we have noticed in the previous chapters, constructions of God in the New Testament writings are influenced by the larger situations or circumstances from which the writings emerge and that they address. That is certainly true for 1 John. While we don't know all the details, we can reconstruct something of a fight in the community that led to a split or division. Some members left:

> They went out from us, but they did not belong to us; for if they had belonged to us, they would have remained with us. But by going out they made it plain that none of them belongs to us. (1 John 2:19)

Who is the writer referring to? In the prior verse, he nastily refers to those who have "gone out" from the community as "antichrists" and later, as "children of the devil" (1 John 3:10) and "false prophets who have gone out into the world" (1 John 4:1). This is polemical language infused with anger and bitterness from the conflict.

What is the fight about? It's difficult to know for sure, but the letter is very combative in attacking certain theological (mis)understandings especially about Jesus. Being an antichrist, for example, means "denying the Father and Son" (1 John 2:22) and denying "that Jesus has come in the flesh" (1 John 3:2-3). There are also attacks about whether sin matters (1 John 1:6–2:2) and repeated exhortations to love others and obey God's commandments.

Whatever the precise details, the letter writer tries to make sense of the conflict and departure of some community members. He does so by constructing a dualistic view of the circumstances that contrasts the good guys and the bad guys. He creates an "us" versus "them" framework that comprises those who come from God (those still in the community) and those who come from the devil (those who have left the community), those who belong to truth and those who exemplify falsehood and error, those who belong to God as God's children and those who are children of the devil and who comprise "the world." The writer posits continuing conflict between the two groups as inevitable, so he emphasizes love for one another within the community to ensure its solidarity, distinctive identity, and mutual support so that others do not leave. He regularly contrasts his loving community with "the world," the rest of society that does not think or believe in the way that his group does and that is marked, he claims, by hate. The writer clearly feels embattled, angry, betrayed, and confused and works hard to differentiate his own group theologically, socially, and cosmically from those whom he deems false antichrists who abandoned the community.

Keeping these circumstances of crisis and division in view helps us to understand some of the ways 1 John constructs God.

God in 1 John 3–4

Chapters 3 and 4 of 1 John, comprising some forty-five verses, mention God thirty-nine times and "Father" twice. Certainly references to Jesus are prominent (some twelve times), and God and Jesus are intertwined in various ways, as they are throughout the letter. Yet there's no doubt that the construction of God centered on love is integral to the chapters. The chapters develop the implications of this construction for the identity and existence of the beleaguered community they address.

The passage begins in 1 John 3:1 by constructing God-at-work as the Father displaying his love in creating "children of God": "See what love the Father has given us, that we should be called children of God; and that is what we are."

First John employs a "spiral" style of writing whereby familiar themes keep circling around, being restated and developed anew. Only one of the previous eight references to God as Father has linked God and love (1 John 2:15). Here verse 1 emphasizes God's initiative in this display of love. It is a gift. It exhibits God "for us," turned toward people and actively creating and embracing them with love and bestowing the identity of children who belong to and originate with God.

This statement, though, is not a universal statement. The writer is not saying that all people are God's children. It is—**Red-flag alert**—a limited statement that applies to and defines his particular group of Jesus-believers who have not left the community: "and that is what we are" (1 John 3:1). The "we" language is crucial. It refers to a group or insider identity that creates a "them" and "us" dualism. It marks the writer's audience of Jesus-believers as a distinct and special group brought into existence by a loving God-at-work.

This community is distinguished from the "world" which the writer describes as those who have not known God and therefore do not recognize or belong to God's children (1 John 3:2b). In not recognizing God, they show, so the writer stereotypically claims, that they are committed to lawlessness and sin (1 John 3:4, 8). This dualism—and the **Red flag** is still waving—is not just social and moral comprising "our" community and the community of all the rest. It is also cosmic. Their nonrecognition of God shows that they are not children of God but children of the devil: "everyone who commits sin is a child of the devil" (1 John 3:8). They are identified by "not doing what is right" and they "do not love their brothers and sisters" (1 John 3:10).

By contrast, the writer makes the strange and disturbing claim that his community, birthed by God the Father, does not sin. "No one who abides in him sins" (1 John 3:6); and "those who have been born of God do not sin because God's seed abides in them; they cannot sin because they have been born of God" (1 John 3:9).

There are, then, according to the author, two procreative forces at work in the world that account for the origin of all people, either God or the devil. This parentage or origin that constitutes two groups of people is made known by how people live (no sin or sin), whether they know God (through Jesus or not), and whether they belong to the writer's community and tradition (loving their brothers and sisters or not). These three criteria provide identity markers for God's children, affirming his community's identity and differentiating them from the rest.

While being loved by God and knowing that one is a child of God is a warm, fuzzy experience and a precious identity, this rigid "them-and-us" scheme is truly a **Red-flag alert**. However, we understand the reasons for the dualism and the circumstances from which it emerges and that it addresses (perhaps a nasty experience of rejection or division), the claim returns us to an issue that has recurred throughout this book. For whom is God God? Is God the God of some people or of all people? Who decides? We have seen texts that struggle with this question in relation to ethnicity (Jews *and* Gentiles?), gender (male *and* female?), social status (elites *and* poor folks) and now religion—all people or only Jesus-believers, and then, those who believe "like us"? Does God play favorites and love only a few people, designating only a few to be God's pets or children? Is much of humanity truly children of the devil? Such a claim dismisses and depersonalizes most of the population and provides a space for oppressive actions. The creation story of Genesis 1 takes a very different approach in seeing all people as the creatures and children of God.

Also disturbing (another **Red-flag moment**) is the notion that children of God (believers in Jesus) are without sin (3:6, 9). That statement is blatantly not true as personal experience and the history of the church confirm. Theologians, for example Charles Wesley, have tried to explain the claim in terms of what is possible when a believer abides in faith and love, in prayer and thanksgiving. While that may be so, such moments do not last for long, as experience teaches us. And the history of the church is fearful and dreadful with sinful actions. The delusion that the church is without sin and always does the will of God has legitimated all sorts of devastating wickedness.

God's Love and Those in Need (1 John 3:11-17)

This next section develops one of the identity markers of being God's children, namely expressing God's love by loving brothers and sisters. The lack of such love was identified in 1 John 3:10 as one of the markers of the children of the devil. Here Cain, who murdered his brother Abel (Gen 4:1-16), is held up as a prime example of one who did not love and thereby shown to have the devil as his father. He was "from the evil one and murdered his brother" because the evil person always hates the good person (1 John 3:12). So, according to the writer, his community of Jesus-believers can expect opposition, violence, even murder from the hateful "children of the devil" or "the world" that surrounds them and in the midst of which they live (1 John 3:13-15). The identity of those who left the community has been expanded to include "everybody" as well as a cosmic force. By contrast, the community of God's children is marked by God's love, which is demonstrated by community members in practical love for those brothers and sisters in need:

> How does God's love abide in anyone who has the world's goods and sees a brother or sister in need and yet refuses help? (1 John 3:17)

We know that people in duress can make wild statements. "I dropped my tray in the cafeteria and the *whole school* laughed at me." So we can perhaps understand why and how this rhetoric in 1 John might come into being. But the rhetoric is now part of Christian scriptures, disconnected from those circumstances of origin, and read as authoritative texts in relation to all sorts of situations. Again the **Red flag** is rightly waving on at least two counts.

First, the writer's claim, reflecting the letter's construction of a dualistic cosmos, that "the world" knows nothing of loving actions but knows only hate and murder, is simply ridiculous. Public responses to natural disasters, to acts of civil violence, to neighbors in need are but three examples of the ability of most human beings to care for each other. And to claim, conversely, that only Jesus-believers know how to express love is also ridiculous. Our human experience exposes these lies every day. The history of the church's involvement with ethnic, sexual, and religious intolerance across the centuries (to name a few instances) also attests to their falseness. The letter's formulation may reflect, and seek to interpret, a particular historical experience of division and conflict that the author was addressing (1 John 2:18-19), but when these claims about God's love or "the world's" behaviors are detached from those circumstances of conflict and generalized to explain all human behaviors for all time, they become very destructive.

And second, we should note how limited is the concern for those in need of the world's goods in 1 John 3:17. The writer's vision extends only to the community of "brothers and sisters." God's love here does not extend to all people in need and certainly not to enemies as it does in the Sermon on the Mount, where God loves indiscriminately and impartially (Matt 5:43-47).

Back to the letter. It's almost as if the writer knows that he has set the bar impossibly high (1 John 3:18-22). While the writer has claimed that "those who have been born of God do not sin" (1 John 3:9), he has also recognized sin previously as a basic reality that must be acknowledged and confessed (1 John 1:8–2:2). Now having exhorted love in action and not just in words, he backs off somewhat to recognize that

> whenever our hearts condemn us, God is greater than our hearts and knows everything. (1 John 3:20)

The only circumstances in which "our hearts condemn us" involves failing to live up to God's standards. So the writer offers assurance that God, who knows everything, is "greater than our hearts" when they condemn his audience for failing to love the brothers and sisters, and when they experience the accompanying self-recriminations, guilt, shame, or doubt. The "heart" signifies human conscience, willing, knowing, deciding, and doing. Failures and the resultant self-accusation do not, the writer asserts, cancel the identity of being God's children. God-at-work is greater or bigger or more powerful than human failures and self-recriminations. The writer's claim here is very similar to Paul's rhetorical question in Romans 3:3: "Will their faithlessness nullify the faithfulness of God? By no means!" Nor do failures prevent God's children approaching God with "boldness" in prayer and receiving "from him whatever we ask" (1 John 3:22; though it's not always that easy, is it?).[1] The writer's assurance is that God's love continues unabated for God's children even when they fail.

Yet having provided reassurance, the writer's demanding, commanding, authoritative God resurfaces. God has given a double commandment—to believe in "his Son Jesus Christ" and to "love one another"

(1 John 3:23). These commandments are to be obeyed—and clearly those who have left the community have not done so. But the reward for the insiders, the children of God, from such obedience is immense. It comprises not just encounters with a commanding God but mutual abiding with God: "All who obey his commandments abide in him, and he abides in them" (1 John 3:24). Here the construction of God changes considerably. This language of "abiding in" denotes the most intimate and mystical union with God in which God and the person indwell one another. The image affirms God's accessibility to people and desire to be in intimate relationship and encounter. "Abiding in" is the writer's favorite language (for example 1 John 2:24, 27; 3:6, 17; 4:12-16). But the price for not "abiding" is huge and horrible.

Discerning Spirits (1 John 4:1-6)

Such indwelling occurs through the Holy Spirit, which God has given to God's children (1 John 3:24). In this indwelling, God utilizes particular human agents to communicate on God's behalf with people. But the writer is aware that among those who claim to belong to the community of Jesus-believers are "false prophets" who claim to be inspired by God's Spirit when they speak (1 John 4:1). How does the audience distinguish between the true and bogus words and separate the fake prophet from the genuine? How does the community adjudicate the claim to be moved or possessed by the Spirit of God? The content of the speaker's confession provides the criterion: "Every spirit that confesses that Jesus Christ has come in the flesh is from God" (1 John 4:2b-3a). This confession affirms the significance of Jesus's activity on God's behalf as a human being among human beings.

The key issue concerning the true or false prophets involves "origin." Where one comes from determines who one is; origin shapes identity and destiny. Again the writer develops a dualism, this time between two spirits, one of truth and one of error (1 John 4:6). False prophets who do not make an adequate confession about Christ (that Jesus has come in the flesh; 1 John 4:2) speak by "the spirit of the antichrist" (1 John 4:3). They are "from the world," opponents of God, so they get a good hearing in the world which reveals their falseness (1 John 4:5). By contrast, the children of God "are from God" (1 John 4:4, 6) who is greater than the world. By contrast, "we" get a good hearing among those who are also from God. Response to the respective proclamations functions to reveal who are children of God and who are not.

Red-flag alert: Is it necessary to identify everyone who disagrees with a religious community as an agent of the devil?

God Is Love (1 John 4:7-21)

The writer continues to emphasize "love for one another" (1 John 4:7) but does so by developing the link between love for others and God's love. Verses 7 and 8 assert a rich mix of claims. The writer repeats the priority of God's love. Love belongs to and originates with God since the very being of God is love. God's love is active and fertile. The love of God-at-work, mother-like, produces children. The mark of the identity of these children (those who belong to God and are born from and by God) is that they imitate the very being of God in loving deeds. This love ensures these children encounter or know God. By contrast, those who do not love do not know God. Love originates from God because God is love:

> Because love is from God, everyone who loves is born of God and knows God. Whoever does not love does not know God for God is love. (1 John 4:7-8).

From the priority of God's active and powerful love, the writer moves to its revelation. This revelation takes place not in some vague way but in a historical person and his activity, namely in God's son Jesus whom God sends to be "an atoning sacrifice for our sins" (1 John 4:10). As with Paul's letter to the church in Rome (Rom 5:8; see ch. 12 above), the writer amazingly sees Jesus's death by crucifixion (as God-forsaken an event as can be imagined), as a display of God's love. The powerful love of God-at-work is not averted or overwhelmed by, but embraces, human rejection. Again the priority of the love of God-at-work is asserted: "In this is love, not that we loved God but that he loved us and sent his Son to be the atoning sacrifice for our sins" (1 John 4:10).

This revelation of God's love in Jesus's death functions as both a model and a source of empowerment for God's children to "love one another."

In the exercise of love for another, the God whom no one "has ever seen" is made visible and present: "God lives in us and his love is perfected in us" (1 John 4:12). Acts of love for another person render God present and complete God's love thereby forming a community of indwelling and mutual intimacy: "God is love, and those who abide in love abide in God and God abides in them" (1 John 4:16).

For the writer of 1 John, the very essence of God is love, not anger, judgment, vindictiveness, or indifference. Beyond the present and the loving experience of the presence of God, this love—however only for God's children—extends to the future "day of judgment" where "we may have boldness" and "there is no fear in love but perfect love casts out fear" (1 John 4:17-18). All of these claims demarcate the writer's community over against the outsiders who have left the community and are presented as being beyond the reach of the love of God and God's children.

The final verses return to the theme of love for brothers and sisters but now emphasize that God is not just the origin of that love but also its object (1 John 4:19-21). For the third time, the writer emphasizes the priority of God's love and its impact in effecting one-another love: "we love because he first loved us" (1 John 4:19). Verse 20 moves from God as the cause of this love to the object of human love. To love God requires love for the brothers and sisters. One without the other is impossible:

> Those who say, "I love God," and hate their brothers and sisters are liars; for those who do not love a brother or sister whom they have seen cannot love God whom they have not seen. (1 John 4:20)

Presumably the jibe here concerns those who have abandoned the writer's community, a definitive gesture of not loving the brothers and sisters.

Again there is a **Red-flag alert**. The absolute declarations and "us-and-them" boundaries reflect the writer's situation of conflict and polemic. Human experience, as we know, is not as clean-cut and not as easily catalogued as the writer suggests. Nor is the love of God.

The writer's circumstances clearly impact the constructions of God in these two chapters. I have indicated in the discussion above that there is a considerable shadow side to the writer's dualistic formulations arising out of his specific situation, especially when those claims are detached from the situation of conflict and read as general statements about God and about human beings. Yet, it is also true that, as so often happens, much truth about God and about life lived in relation to God-at-work emerges in desperate circumstances. Some of the writer's affirmations have become bedrock commitments in the Christian tradition. That God-at-work is love—and not hate or indifference—is one such statement. So too is the notion of God's accessibility and relationality expressed in the image of mutual abiding or indwelling. Also vital has been the connection between commitment to God and practical love for other human beings.

Questions for Reflection/Discussion

1. Do you agree that there are reasons to be troubled by some of the claims about God in 1 John 3–4? Identify some of these challenges. How much does understanding something of the circumstances of the community addressed by the letter help to account for some of these claims? What dangers arise if these circumstances are neglected? Can you think of circumstances when some of these claims might seem inappropriate or harmful?

2. What for you are the strengths or valuable affirmations about God that the two chapters make?

3. Several verses here indicate God as Father producing children (1 John 3:1, 9). Consider some other biblical images of God as a woman: Luke 15:8-10; Deuteronomy 32:11-12, 18; Isaiah 42:13-15; 49:14-15; 66:13; Hosea 11:3-4; 13:8.

Further Reading

Raymond Brown, *The Community of the Beloved Disciple: The Life, Loves, and Hates of an Individual Church in New Testament Times* (New York: Paulist, 1979), 93–144, 166–67 (a classic discussion).

Warren Carter and Amy-Jill Levine, *The New Testament: Methods and Meanings* (Nashville: Abingdon, 2013), 327–40.

Chapter 16
God on the Throne (Rev 19:1-10; 21:1-8)

> Read Revelation 19:1-10; 21:1-8 before reading this chapter. Then refer to these passages while you read the chapter.

Everybody has an opinion about the book of Revelation. Some people can't live without it; some people can't live with it. Some people think it weird; some people think it wonderful. Some people wish it left behind; others think it predicts next year's news long before the TV networks and Internet get hold of it. Among all its strange beasts, numbers, palettes of colors, symbols, and focus on Jesus, are some very important, very big, and ambivalent constructions of God-at-work. We will focus on two scenes from the last section of Revelation, which reveal God as ruler and God of God's new world.

A Structured Revelation: God-at-Work as the Ruler of All

Revelation is not a random book. It is tightly structured with a series of revelations that lead to the disclosure of God-at-work in the whole world in these final chapters as ruler and God. Its vision is international and cosmic. It begins with revelations or theological perspectives on seven local churches and on its contemporary Roman Empire before envisioning God's rule victoriously established over all nations and all creation.

- The book begins by making an authority claim. In a context of conflict among communities of Jesus-believers about how to engage their imperial world, the document declares it reveals God's will (ch. 1). Some in the seven churches will accept this claim, others will not.

- Then in a series of seven short letters to seven churches in the province of Asia (present-day Turkey), and in a context of conflict and disagreement, the document reveals that cultural accommodation or fitting in with the practices and priorities of the Roman Empire is contrary to God's purposes (chs. 2–3). Again some will accept this claim while others will reject it.

- Then the document offers six reasons as to why involvement in the world of Rome's empire is contrary to God's will.

- Chapters 4–5 reveal that true worship and allegiance belong only to God and God's son Jesus as the creator and redeemer.

- Further, it reveals that God is not pleased with the current Roman world. The empire is imploding under judgment from its greedy and violent strategies (chs. 6–8).

- God, however, is giving the empire a chance to repent (chs. 8–11).

- But the chances are not good because, the writer reveals, the empire is in the control of the devil (chs. 12–14).

- True to form, he reveals that the empire's time is up as God judges and destroys the eternal empire (chs. 15–18).

- In its place, Revelation reveals, God establishes God's own rule over the whole world (chs. 19–22).[1]

Within this last section, Revelation 19:1-10 offers a heavenly scene depicting worship of God. It is not the first such scene in Revelation. Worship and its related issues of loyalty and commitments are a major theme throughout the book. These issues of loyalty emerge in the letters of chapters 2–3 written to seven churches in cities in the province of Asia. The writer complains that the churches are too accommodated to their imperial society, practicing what he calls "fornication and eating food sacrificed to idols" (Rev 2:14, 20). The word "fornication" usually refers to some kinds of illicit sexual activity, but along with other sexual metaphors (such as adultery and prostitution) it commonly refers in the scriptures, as here, to false worship and involvement with idols (Ps 106:34-39; Jer 3:6-10). Food sold in marketplaces and available at various civic and group feasts had often been dedicated to deities. Some Jesus-believers were participating in gatherings where idols were honored and food previously offered to idols was consumed. Perhaps they justified this participation by arguing, as Paul does in 1 Corinthians 8:4-6, that no idol really exists and "for us there is one God." If idols have no reality, eating food that has been offered to them and being present when offerings were made to idols did not matter. Honoring idols and images of the emperor was not compulsory but "everybody did it" as an expression of loyalty and a means of evoking the gods' favor on their city and empire.

The writer, however, does not agree with them. He demands in the letters of chapters 2–3 that Jesus-believers absent themselves from these practices. In chapter 13, he makes the startling revelation that the devil is behind these worship practices. The elites in provincial cities such as the seven cities addressed in chapters 2 and 3 who encourage such worship are agents of the devil (13:11-18). This revelation sets up a cosmic struggle between God and the devil, between true worship and false worship, between true Jesus-believers and false ones, between those loyal to the writer of Revelation and those loyal to church leaders such as the woman he names "Jezebel" in Thyatira who supports participation (Rev 2:18-29).

His argument is that if the Jesus-believers understand the devilish forces at work behind these everyday cultural practices and structures, then they will not have anything to do with them. Why would Jesus-believers want to be compromised by involvement in something devilish? Worship reflects the commitments and a way of life of the worshipper and raises the question of the worthiness of what or who is worshipped. Only God is worthy of worship.

"Jezebel"

The writer is especially vicious in his attack on the leader of the church in Thyatira (Rev 2:28-29). He nicknames her "Jezebel" after the wife of King Ahab. Ahab and Jezebel led Israel into worshipping the god Baal (1 Kgs 16:29-33). The writer accuses "Jezebel" of making herself a prophet (instead of being called to be a prophet by God), of deceiving the people (the devil's task in Rev 12:9) and says she teaches "the deep things of Satan" (Rev 2:20, 24).

Clearly there is a major conflict. Why is he so opposed to her? Perhaps he thinks a woman should not lead a church. More likely, he disagrees with her teaching that Jesus-followers should engage the imperial world, rather than retreat from it as the writer urges them to do. If this is the issue at stake, we can speculate on what she might have been teaching. Perhaps the folks in her congregation struggled for survival and had no option but to be engaged in daily economic activities. Perhaps she had concluded from the previous martyrdom of Antipas (Rev 2:13) that refusal to participate in civic honoring and socioeconomic activities created suspicion and risked a violent backlash that was unnecessary. Perhaps she agreed with Paul's arguments in 1 Corinthians 8 that idols had no existence and posed no threat. Perhaps she saw in the scriptures examples of people like Joseph and Jeremiah who cooperated with imperial power. Perhaps she did not see the empire in the hands of the devil. Rather, perhaps she agreed with those that interpreted Rome's defeat of Jerusalem in 70 CE as a sign of God's blessing on Rome. We don't know any of this for sure, but "Jezebel" may well have had some strong arguments for involvement in daily societal life.

Clearly John does not agree. But—**Red-flag alert**—his rhetoric toward her is disturbingly, regrettably, and unnecessarily abusive and violent (Rev 2:23-24). There are other negative presentations of women in Revelation, which must not be understood as justifying derogatory or violent treatment of women.

The writer makes the point that only God is to be worshipped again in chapter 4 but by different means. In chapter 4, he offers a contrasting vision of the heavens in which true worship is underway. At the center is God on the throne, a common Hebrew Bible symbol for God's power and rule: "I saw the Lord sitting on a throne, high and lofty; and the hem of his robe filled the temple" (Isa 6:1; also Ezek 1:26).

Revelation 4 sets up a dazzling, heavenly throne room scene. The colors of precious stones evoke God's magnificence (Rev 4:3a). A rainbow recalls God's mercy and faithfulness to Noah (Rev 4:3b). Lightning and thunder indicate God's power and presence in creation (Rev 4:5). Seven torches represent seven spirits by which God-at-work operates in the world (Rev 4:5b). And "something like a sea of glass" denotes God's control over the chaotic sea (Rev 4:6). These elements underscore God's power, mercy, faithfulness, action, and splendor.

Also in the throne room are some living beings who worship God, namely twenty-four elders (Rev 4:4, 10) and four creatures representing all creation in the form of wild animals (lion), domesticated animals (ox), birds (eagle), and human beings (Rev 4:6-8). "Day and night without ceasing," these creatures worship, acknowledging God's power as "the Almighty" and God's eternal existence as the one who spans all time past, present, and future (Rev 4:8). At the same time, the twenty-four elders acknowledge God as worthy to receive "glory, honor and power" because God has "created all things" (Rev 4:11). God is worthy to be worshipped because God created the world and has a claim of ownership on it that God's creatures should acknowledge. From chapter 4's focus on worshipping God as the creator, chapter 5 continues the worship but now with the focus on Jesus who is celebrated for his role in effecting salvation.

The point the writer makes in chapters 4–5 is that true worship belongs to God the creator and Jesus the redeemer. It is not to be compromised in any way by involvement with idols and imperial honoring. The writer offers a vision of this true worship already underway in the heavens to encourage his audience to participate in it and distance themselves from imperial ways.

The writer continues to keep scenes of God being worshipped in the heavens in front of his audience by inserting them at regular intervals throughout the document. They function like variations on a theme with each scene offering a different emphasis. In Revelation 7:9-17, for example, the focus falls on a worshipping multinational crowd. This "great multitude . . . from every nation, from all tribes and people and languages" acknowledges that "salvation belongs to our God who is seated on the throne . . . blessing and glory and wisdom and thanksgiving and honor and power and might be to our God forever and ever" (Rev 7:10-12). In their worship, this international crowd honors and gives thanks to God for God's blessing, wisdom, and power.

Or as another example, the worship scene in 11:15-19 anticipates the scene in 19:1-10 by celebrating the victory of God's reign over the Roman Empire: "The kingdom of the world has become the kingdom of our Lord . . . and he will reign forever and ever" (Rev 11:15).

Again God is addressed as the Almighty, thereby emphasizing God's unrivalled power that is constructed as being victorious over Rome's empire: "We give you thanks, Lord God Almighty . . . for you have taken your great power and begun to reign" (Rev 11:17).

Not everybody, though, is happy with God-at-work asserting God's rule. In particular, the nations allied with Rome struggle against God's rule but in vain: "The nations raged, but your wrath has come, and the time . . . for rewarding your servants . . . and for destroying those who destroy the earth" (Rev 11:18). The scope of God's activity is extensive. God subdues the Roman Empire and the nations by asserting God's empire.

A subsequent worship scene moves beyond the celebration of subduing the nations to a different focus. God is again "the Almighty" one of great power with sovereignty exercised over the nations as "King of the nations" (Rev 15:3). In this scene, though, surprisingly, "all nations will come and worship before you" (Rev 15:4). The image is not of nations subjugated but nations turned toward God in worship. Again God is addressed in terms of great power that accomplishes God's purposes as the "Almighty" as well as the "King of the nations" (Rev 15:3).

God on the Throne (Rev 19:1-10; 21:1-8)

All of these scenes look forward to God-at-work on an international scale. They anticipate God dealing not with individuals but with nations and empires over whom God is victorious.

The scene in chapter 19, by contrast, does not look forward to what God will do but looks back on what God has achieved in bringing Rome's empire to an end. The heavenly crowd worships God with *Hallelujah*, a Hebrew term commonly used in the Psalms and meaning "praise God." They acknowledge God's "salvation and glory and power." Salvation here refers to God's victory over Rome who is presented with some negative gender and sexual imagery as corrupting the world: "because he has judged the great whore who corrupted the earth with her fornication" (Rev 19:2).

God's power is immense in bringing down the mighty empire that was to last forever (*Roma aeterna*). But now, instead, from her ruins, "the smoke goes up from her forever and ever" (Rev 19:3). The crowd offers its evaluation of God-at-work in removing the world's dominant empire: "for his judgments are true and just" (Rev 19:2).

The two previous chapters have depicted the Roman Empire as "fallen" or destroyed by God-at-work. Chapter 17—**Red-flag alert**— presents Rome as a "whore" or prostitute, a wicked and faithless city. The personification occurs in the Hebrew Bible for cities like Jerusalem (Ezek 16; 23) and Tyre (Isa 23:15-17) and presents them as judged to be wicked and faithless. While the image was traditional, its use is disturbing for contemporary readers because of its negative presentation of women. The image continues that of *fornication* or illicit sexual activity used in chapters 2–3 to represent faithless participation in the Roman Empire. Here in Revelation 17:2, Rome's allies and client kings are said to commit fornication or have sex with the prostitute Rome. The image refers to their socioeconomic, cultural, military, and political cooperation with Rome. Verse 4 describes her extravagant and luxurious clothing, which represents Rome's wealth gained by exploitative taxation, tribute, and trade.

Chapter 18 announces Rome's fall. The first eight and the final five verses (Rev 18:1-8, 20-24) declare God has destroyed Babylon/Rome: "for her sins are heaped high as heaven, and God has remembered her iniquities" (18:5). These sins are primarily identified as economic excess and luxury (Rev 18:3, 7). Her judgment comprises "pestilence and mourning and famine . . . and fire; for mighty is the Lord God who judges her" (Rev 18:8). The rest of the chapter mocks three groups who were integral to and beneficiaries of Roman power—client or puppet kings (Rev 18:9), merchants (Rev 18:11), shipmasters and sailors (Rev 18:17)—who mourn or lament the empire's destruction.

Chapter 19 celebrates God's accomplishment of destroying the empire. Verse 2 salutes God's accomplishments as "judgments that are true and just." As readers, we of course are supposed to join in the celebrations. But there's a **Red-flag alert**. The scene constructs God as a powerful Roman emperor or general—on steroids! In chapter 18, God is envisioned as behaving just like them in violently destroying the city of Rome. Recall that the city of Jerusalem and its temple were burned in 70 CE under the general and soon-to-be emperor Titus. The writer constructs God as imitating the ways of Caesar in acting violently and punishing those who have not yielded to God's ways.

Meantime the twenty-four elders and four living creatures—first introduced in the heavenly worship scene of chapter 4—join the "great multitude" in the hallelujah session and fall down to worship God (Rev 19:4). A cheerleading voice from the throne exhorts everyone to worship (Rev 19:5). The crowd responds with more hallelujahs and recognitions of God's power and rule.

But there's a new piece, another female image: "For the marriage of the Lamb has come and his bride has made herself ready" (Rev 19:7). This image in which the heavenly crowd comprises the bride for the Lamb (Jesus crucified and risen in ch. 5) builds on the Hebrew Bible theme in which Israel is the (often faithless) bride of God (Hos 2:19-20; Ezek 16). But the Lamb's bride is clothed with "fine linen, bright and pure" and marked by "righteous deeds"—all in contrast to Rome the whore. This "bride" vs. "prostitute" binary using female figures to represent "good and bad" is surely disturbing for contemporary readers. An angel adds a beatitude, blessing those who "are invited to the marriage supper of the Lamb" (Rev 19:9). This "marriage supper" evokes the scene in Isaiah 25, which presents God hosting a meal "for all peoples" at which God establishes salvation on earth. Salvation comprises the ending of hunger, all pain, tears, and death (Isa 25:6-10a).

The writer is so excited by the angel's blessing that he impulsively breaks his rigid no-worship-for-anyone-other-than-God rule and falls down to worship the angel! That's a nice comedic touch in a rather intense book! The angel rebukes the writer and preaches to him as the wayward choir—"Worship God" (Rev 19:10).

God's New City

After a series of six visions of God's rule through chapters 19–20, chapter 21 offers a seventh vision that centers on God's new and splendid city, the new Jerusalem, that contrasts condemned and destroyed Rome (chs. 17–18). The writer sees a "new heaven and a new earth," a transformation of, not a replacement for, God's good creation. There's no place for the sea, traditionally a place of chaos but now subject to God's purposes and rule (Rev 21:1). The new Jerusalem descends "out of heaven from God" (21:2). It is God's gift and work; it is not a human achievement. It is hailed as God's home or tabernacle "among mortals" (21:3). There is no special house for God such as a temple (Rev 21:22). God is present with and among people. The writer cites a form of Ezekiel 37:27 that employs covenant language: "He will dwell with them; they will be his peoples; and God himself will be with them" (Rev 21:3). There is a significant change in the citation. Ezekiel's language of "people" referring to Israel has been changed from the singular form to the plural "peoples." The plural expands one nation into many, denoting the international inhabitants of the new city centered on God and living in faithful communion with God.

God has also transformed the living conditions in this new city:

> He will wipe away every tear from their eyes. Death will be no more; mourning and crying and pain will be no more, for the first things have passed away." (Rev 21:4)

In God's new city, there will be no tears, no death, no mourning, no crying, and no pain. God removes suffering, brokenness, and decay as

God-at-work renovates or transforms the present world and makes "all things new" (Rev 21:4-5).

This is the goal or "end" of God's work. The creator completes his purposes initiated from the beginning in creation. Using the first and last letters of the Greek alphabet, God declares: "I am the Alpha and the Omega, the beginning and the end" (21:6). God had introduced himself as "the Alpha and the Omega . . . the Almighty" at the beginning of Revelation (1:8). God's power creates, renews, and completes.

As part of this renewing work, God sustains and nourishes this renewed world and life in it with "water as a gift from the spring of the water of life" (Rev 21:6). And consistent with this construction of God as giving and sustaining life, God promises those who share in God's victory to be faithful to them as their parent or father: "I will be their God and they will be my children" (21:7). But there will be no place for the "cowardly, the faithless, the polluted, the murderers, the fornicators, the sorcerers, the idolaters [of course!], and all liars" (Rev 21:8). Apparently these ones are beyond the reach and power of God's renewing presence.

Another **Red flag** blows in the breeze. The final construction of God that Revelation offers is God as the victor over the Roman Empire, an imitator of imperial power and violence, one who out-Caesars Caesar. But beyond this, God's new world is an empire that God rules over as emperor (Rev 5:10; 11:15). While the nations come to worship God (Rev 15:4) and while the nations will bring their "honor" to worship God (Rev 21:24-26), there is no tolerance for dissenters, for those who do not toe the party line. Is God's empire as coercive as that of the Romans?

Questions for Reflection/Discussion

1. According to Revelation, what is God doing in the world? Compare Isaiah 25:6-10a and Revelation 21:1-8.

2. There are some troubling dimensions of the constructions of God in Revelation: the use of violence, imitation of the empire, and the depictions of women. How do we as contemporary readers of scripture make sense of such presentations?

God on the Throne (Rev 19:1-10; 21:1-8)

3. Revelation raises the difficult question of how contemporary Jesus-believers might relate to and engage their surrounding cultures and society. The writer of Revelation urges distance and retreat (18:4). Is this a satisfactory or even workable option? Jezebel offers an alternative of thoughtful engagement. How might contemporary believers negotiate this task?

4. In God's new empire, who will be oppressed, marginalized, or exploited?

Further Reading

Warren Carter, *What Does Revelation Reveal? Unlocking the Mystery* (Nashville: Abingdon, 2011)—an excellent study book.

Wes Howard-Brook and Anthony Gwyther, *Unveiling Empire: Reading Revelation Then and Now* (Maryknoll, NY: Orbis, 2001).

Chapter 17

Conclusion?

Conclusions usually sum up the argument of the book. They pull the various pieces together, make them all fit into one big whole, and put a cute little bow on top. But as I said in chapter 1, I was not looking for the New Testament texts that I have discussed to produce one neat image of God in which all the pieces happily come together. I don't think that's possible partly because the NT texts don't speak of God in one voice, and partly because we've looked at a sample of only fifteen texts. There are many more texts in the NT that we could look at. Our results are messy rather than neat.

So in this "conclusion," I want to think about two questions that have been lurking around this study: What ways of talking about God have we observed in the NT writings, and what constructions of God result? The two questions are of course connected, but each dimension is worth foregrounding.

Ways of Talking About God

Our fifteen sample texts provide a wide range of ways of talking about God. I have identified seven categories. First, our sample includes several *narratives* with each one employing different ways of talking about God. The Acts 10–11 narrative involving Cornelius and Peter constructs God as very interventionist and directive (ch. 9 above). The narrative employs more than thirty-five instances in which God intervenes through visions, prayers, trances, the Holy Spirit, angels, and the divine voice. God is up front and in your face in this narrative. Likewise in the healing of the paralyzed man, God's miraculous power is narrated as interventionist and transformative for effecting the man's healing (John 5; ch. 8 above). By contrast, in Matthew 1–2 (ch. 2 above), God is mentioned just a few times, apparently more absent than present, yet I suggested that in various ways the chapters constantly evoke God's activity. The narrative of Mark 1 (ch. 4 above) emphasizes Jesus as God's agent acting on God's behalf, commissioned by God ("Christ," "Son of God," "my Son the Beloved"), and attested by Isaiah and John the Baptist to announce and perform the "good news of God" and "the kingdom/empire/reign" of God.

As a second way of talking about God, the Gospel texts employ *parables*. Parables create comparisons or analogies, setting a situation or narrative action in relation to God or God's reign. Parables employ an "is like to" or "may be compared to" approach whereby statements about God are linked to human situations and experiences that picture something of God-at-work. The parable of Matthew 22:1-14 (ch. 3 above) sets "the kingdom of heaven" in relation to a scenario of a king inviting guests to the wedding banquet of his son. God is constructed as behaving like the king. In Luke 11 (ch. 7 above), God engaged in prayer is compared to two household situations, one involving a neighbor and hospitality and one involving a parent providing a child with a healthy snack. Both situations work on a "how much more" principle. If humans know how to behave generously, how much more does God.

A third way of talking about God involves *sustained verbal proclamations or speeches* made on God's behalf by key figures. Jesus proclaims and performs "the good news about/from God" and the kingdom/reign of God" (Mark 1:14-15; ch. 4 above), declares particular human situations and groups that God blesses and condemns (Luke 6; ch. 6 above), and announces the love of the Father for the Son and all that the Father has delegated to the Son (judging, giving life; John 5:19-30; ch. 8 above). Paul proclaims "the power of God into salvation" as well as "the wrath of God" against sin (Rom 1:16-32; ch. 11 above). Subsequently, he proclaims the love of God from which nothing "in all creation" can separate people and which embraces all people, Jews and Gentiles (Rom 8; 11; ch. 12 above).

Conclusion?

And the Paul of Acts proclaims to the Athenian council that God "is not far from each one of us" (Acts 17:27; ch. 9 above). Proclamations don't attempt to present a full and fair presentation; they present what fits the situation and the writer/speaker's argument.

A fourth way of talking about God employs *dualistic or conflictual modes of speech* whereby God is contrasted with or set over against a competing but disparaged entity. So the Gospels' presentations of God's purposes for Jesus emphasize conflict with the power of King Herod (Matt 1–2; ch. 2 above) and of the Jerusalem-based leadership allied with Rome (Mark 14–15; John 5; chs. 5 and 8 above). The Paul of Acts sets the "God who made the world and everything in it" over against idols "formed by the art and imagination of mortals" Acts 17:29; ch. 10 above). The author of James contrasts friendship with God and friendship with the world to which God is opposed; the latter represents the values, practices, and structures of the elite-benefitting imperial status quo that remains neglectful of the vulnerable (ch. 14 above). The writer of 1 John constructs God over against the devil, with the loving children that God has fathered at odds with the hating children fathered by the devil (1 John 3–4; ch. 15 above). In these dualisms and conflicts, God is always presented as the superior option. By contrast, the author of 1 and 2 Timothy abandons a conflictual, dualistic, and "over-against" approach. He adopts a much more imitative strategy of "fitting-into" society whereby God replicates the basic hierarchical and male-centered household structures of the ancient world and is constructed as a house owner who sanctions male leadership (ch. 13 above).

A fifth way of talking about God involves *various forms of expressions associated with worship*. On the cross, Mark's Jesus cries out, quoting the opening line of a lament psalm, accusing the absent yet present God of abandoning him ("My God, My God why have you forsaken me?" Mark 15:34; ch. 5 above). The newly pregnant Mary sings a song of praise to God that celebrates God's favor and intervention in human affairs on behalf of the lowly and oppressed and against the rich and powerful (Luke 1:46-56; ch. 6 above). Jesus teaches his disciples a prayer that requests God to act in particular ways: hallowing God's name, establishing God's reign, supplying daily bread, forgiving sins, and not testing people (Luke 11; ch. 7 above). Paul declares that God's mercy embraces all people, Jews and Gentiles, but just when we are hoping for an explanation of how this might be, Paul switches from proclamation to worship, from explanation to mystery, from discourse to doxology ("To him be the glory forever!" Rom 11:25-36; ch. 12 above). First and Second Timothy often use statements of confession and praise to sanction human actions (ch. 13 above). The writer of Revelation inserts scenes of heavenly worship that, in contrast to worship of idols, construct God variously as creator, as the God of an international community, as victorious over the Roman Empire, and as the one who establishes God's good and loving reign, which removes imperial power, sin, and death (Rev 19:1-10; 21:1-8; ch. 16 above).

A sixth way of talking about God involves the use of *beatitudes, woes, and maxims*. Beatitudes and woes are short statements that make general assertions about the often unexpected or unusual ways in which God is at work. So God blesses and rewards the poor, the hungry, the mourners, and the hated. Conversely, God curses the rich, the full, the laughing, and the complacent (Luke 6:20-26; ch. 6 above). Maxims similarly assert generalities about engagement with God—"therefore whoever wishes to be a friend of the world becomes an enemy of God"; "submit yourselves therefore to God" (Jas 4:4, 7; ch. 14 above).

And a seventh way of talking about God in the New Testament writings concerns the *frequent evoking of the Hebrew Bible by key terms or citations*. This way of talking contextualizes and elaborates claims in the NT writings. Matthew presents a selective review of God-at-work through Israel's history in the form of a genealogy. Then the Gospel employs five citations from various Hebrew Bible writings that interpret the significance of narrative moments (Matt 1–2; ch. 2 above). Mark's presentation of Jesus's central proclamation of "the kingdom of God" evokes Hebrew Bible emphases on God as king and ruler (Mark 1:15; ch. 4 above). On the cross, Jesus quotes Psalm 22:1, thereby presenting himself in relation to a present and absent God (Mark 15:34; ch. 5 above). Mary's song of praise evokes other Hebrew Bible songs of praise offered by the lowly, such as Hannah's song in 1 Samuel 2:1-10 (Luke 1:47-57; ch. 6 above).

John's Jesus argues with the Jerusalem leadership over God's purposes for the Sabbath (John 5; ch. 8 above). Paul in both Romans 1 and Acts 17 draws on Hebrew Bible traditions against idolatry (chs. 10 and 11 above). First Timothy's identification of the church as "the house/hold of God" evokes traditions about the Jerusalem temple (ch. 13 above) and James's insistence on God's favor for the poor draws on prophetic declarations of God's advocacy for the poor and opposition to the rich and powerful (ch. 14 above).

The NT writers employ at least these seven ways of talking about God. What sorts of God do they construct? To repeat, I am not trying to build a composite image of God but noticing some common features among some of the texts as well as some dissimilarities. I will limit the discussion to the fifteen texts considered in the previous chapters. I make three observations.

Constructions of God

The first observation about the NT constructions of God is very obvious, namely that the NT writers construct God in many different ways. Often these diverse presentations conflict with one another and the texts make no effort to smooth out these contradictions that occur either within texts or between texts.

So, for example, Matthew's first two chapters present a God who is very purposeful and intentional in relation to Jesus. Subsequently in the parable of the wedding feast for the king's son, God is simultaneously very generous and gracious, as well as harsh, violent, and judgmental (Matt 22). In Mark, the good news of God and God's rule manifested through Jesus results in life-changing healings, exorcisms, feedings, proclamations, inclusive community, and opposition from the power group based in the temple of Jerusalem. The crucified Jesus, an event that is a political inevitability, addresses in his cry from the cross a paradoxical God who is absent yet present. In Mary's song and Jesus's beatitudes, woes, and prayer, Luke's Gospel constructs God-at-work actively condemning and turning imperial societal structures upside down, siding with the vulnerable and poor against the powerful and rich. John's God judges and gives life through his agent Jesus. The God of Acts is very interventionist in ensuring the inclusion of Gentiles along with Jews, but very "jealous" or intolerant when it comes to the worship of idols. Paul celebrates "the power of God into salvation" that expresses God's righteousness or faithfulness along with announcing the wrath of God in which God avenges human dishonoring of God. Subsequently, his focus moves to the love of God from which nothing separates people and to the powerful mercy of God that embraces Jew and Gentile.

While these presentations see God actively at work in the world transforming and saving it, the writers of 1 and 2 Timothy see God much more at home in this world, imitating its central structure of the household and upholding a basic structure of patriarchy. James, though, creates a dualism or societal antithesis between God, who is on the side of the poor and vulnerable, and "the world" of Roman imperial, hierarchical, and patriarchal structures that favor the elite at the expense of the poor. First John also constructs a dualism but on a cosmic level. The letter presents God as love, but this love seems to reside only in John's community comprising the children of God who are to love one another. It does not seem to extend to God's adversary, the devil, nor to all the rest who are declared to be children of the devil and who major in hate. This God of love seems very limited and sectarian, in contrast, for example, with Paul's God in Romans whose loving mercy is all-encompassing. Revelation envisions God as having resolved these dualistic struggles that James and 1 John, for example, delineate. The new age has already arrived in fullness and judged the present world with God's violent destruction of Rome. The Roman Empire, the "kingdom of the world has become the kingdom of our Lord," and now "the Lord our God the Almighty reigns." For Revelation this creator and re-creator God is worthy of exclusive worship.

The second observation about the NT constructions of God is that across these diverse constructions of God, there is consistent emphasis on God-at-work. The NT texts we have read construct a God who is active in various ways. They do not construct a God who has gone on vacation or given up on planet earth. Rather, these NT texts outline the extent and variety of God-at-work among human beings. I am not suggesting that they all cover the same ground in the same way, but there is some significant overlap. We can note six dimensions of God-at-work. Again, I am not constructing a composite God but noticing six arenas or areas of life in which some of the texts present God-at-work.

The first dimension of God-at-work concerns *cosmic powers*. God conflicts with and overcomes the devil, and demons, the devil's agents. In Mark, God's agent Jesus casts out demons in exorcisms. Paul's cosmic vision of God's love embraces "angels . . . rulers . . . [and] anything else in all creation," none of which, including the devil, can divert God's loving purposes. The dualism that James establishes between God and the world locates the devil in alliance with the latter. Just as James's audience is to befriend God and not the world, so they are to "resist the devil and he will flee from you." In 1 John, God is set over against the devil and the children of God are to discern and resist the activity of false spirits among them as well as children of the devil. Revelation's assertion of the triumph of God's reign means the devil's power is defeated.

A second dimension of God-at-work concerns the creation of the material world. God is the creator who has brought the world into being and seeks to order it. God accomplishes this assertion of God's rule over all things. People are to live as creatures in relation to this creator, not deceiving themselves by creating a false god or idol (Acts; Rom), but acknowledging their creator in worship (Rev).

A third dimension of God-at-work concerns the *ethnic* extent of God's activity that includes Jews and Gentiles. This dimension receives considerable attention across the texts. Matthew's opening genealogy with Abraham and the Babylonian exile, along with the presence of the magi and flight to Egypt, construct God as cosmopolitan. The Acts narrative involving Peter and Cornelius emphasizes Gentile inclusion in God's purposes with its episodic and repetitive style of narration as well as its location within the plan of the larger Acts narrative. Paul explicitly affirms that the one God of Jews and Gentiles extends mercy to all whereby Jews and Gentiles are embraced in God's purposes. Revelation envisions God's reign established over the whole of the creator God's creation, replacing Rome's empire with that of God's. God is commonly constructed as ethnically inclusive.

A fourth dimension of God-at-work concerns *gender*, though the picture here is more muddled. There is no doubt that our NT texts often reflect the patriarchal structures and priorities of their society. In the Gospels, men are more prominent than women and Jesus's disciples are male. There are, of course, scenes in which women are prominent and function as followers of Jesus, yet as I observed in relation to Luke's Gospel, the construction of God is often androcentric. Paul's letter to the Romans, by contrast, recognizes a number of women as coworkers equal with Paul in preaching, church-founding, and pastoral work. By contrast, 1 and 2 Timothy, written in Paul's name by a next-generation disciple, reinscribe patriarchal structures and values. God is constructed as a male house owner and commits leadership of God's house to male leaders with very limited roles for women.

A fifth dimension of God-at-work concerns *societal structures*. Mark presents God's reign manifested in Jesus as positively changing the circumstances of common folks and the vulnerable such as the sick, the demon-possessed, and the hungry. In Luke's Gospel, Mary recognizes God's work in opposing the proud, powerful, and rich while uplifting the lowly and hungry. Jesus's beatitudes similarly see God's work embracing the poor, hungry, mourning, and hated while resisting the rich and full. John's Gospel narrates transforming care expressed to a paralyzed man, but the others at the pool in need of healing disappear from view. James recognizes God's preference for the poor and rejection of societal practice of favoring the rich. The writer of 1 John urges his audience, motivated by God's love, to share their possessions with other brothers and sisters within their community. This concern, though, does not seem to extend beyond the community. Revelation constructs God as violently destroying the elite-benefitting Roman Empire. Concern for the poor is not especially prominent in the selections discussed in the chapters above from Acts, Romans, and 1 and 2 Timothy. And none of our texts shows God resisting the institution of slavery. In fact, in the parable of Matthew 22, in Mary's description of herself as God's slave (Luke 1:48) and in 1 Timothy's presentation of God as the householder, NT texts reinscribe slavery and construct God as slave master.

A sixth dimension of God-at-work concerns *religious practices.* Two questions emerge. We have noted continuities with Israel and Jewish traditions in numerous texts. But Jewish folks, especially the powerful Jerusalem-based societal leaders, are the objects of God's wrath for rejecting God's chosen agent Jesus. So in Matthew's wedding-feast parable, the elites' rejection brings destruction on Jerusalem. In John 5, the same leaders (called "the Jews") plan to put Jesus to death because they think he violates Sabbath and makes himself equal to God. To reject Jesus is to be rejected by the God of Jesus. Yet Paul sees God's mercy embracing "all Israel."

The second question concerns the construction of God in relation to the idols of the nations. Where this issue emerges, these NT texts continue the Hebrew Bible construction of a jealous God who has no patience with worship of idols. Paul in Romans describes God's wrath against those who have made idols, thereby dishonoring God by ignoring the creator-creature relationship. And the Paul of Acts 17 ends his speech about the "unknown god" in Athens by telling his audience that God has tolerated their "ignorance" in the past but time has run out. The letters in Revelation 2–3 show some disagreements about idols in the seven churches with some believers, for example in the church in Thyatira led by the so-called Jezebel, apparently regarding idols to be of no account and so participating freely in their daily imperial society much to the sharp disapproval of the writer of Revelation.

A seventh dimension of God-at-work concerns God *forming communities of people* who encounter God through Jesus. In Matthew 1, the angel names the baby "Jesus" because he will "save his people from their sins." The first thing Mark's Jesus does after announcing God's reign is to call four disciples to encounter that reign in following him. Luke teaches these disciples their own identity-marking prayer. The Cornelius-Peter story in Acts 10–11 establishes this community as comprising Jews and Gentiles, an emphasis that Paul reiterates in Romans. The author of 1 Timothy constructs it as a household. 1 John names it as comprising God's children in distinction from the children of the devil. And Revelation envisions a huge international community of worshippers of God, which has been victorious over the Roman Empire.

These NT texts, then, generally construct God as active in the world. God-at-work is operative in relation to at least seven arenas of life: cosmic powers, the creation, ethnicity, gender, societal structures, religious practices, and forming communities of followers of Jesus.

Red-Flag Alerts

While some of the constructions of God that we have noticed in these NT texts are awe-inspiring or comforting ("God is love"), others are decidedly troubling. I have signaled some of these in the discussions above by calling them **Red-flag alerts**. Here's a sample of some disturbing aspects of these NT constructions of God:

- **God is constructed as very violent.** Like an imperial tyrant, God destroys cities and the Jerusalem elite (Matt 22). He brings down rulers and the wealthy (Luke 1). When dishonored, he expresses his wrath against people (Rom 1). He destroys empires (Rev 18–21). Such a construction of God as violent matters. A recent study has "found compelling evidence that exposure to a scriptural depiction of violence or to violence authorized by a deity can cause readers to behave more aggressively . . . People who believe that God sanctions violence are more likely than others to behave aggressively themselves."[1]

- **God is constructed as neglectful.** God is so focused on protecting the infant Jesus from Herod's envy that a whole bunch of little boys die as collateral damage. Does God not care about the rest? God's healing power makes a paralyzed man walk again, but what about all the other damaged bodies desperately wanting healing at the pool? Was the paralyzed man just a visual aid for a larger theological point? Does God not care about the others?

- **God is constructed as intolerant of other gods.** God has no patience with other religious expressions involving idols (Rom 1; Acts 17). God does not seem to enjoy religious diversity.

- **God is constructed in places as rejecting Jewish leaders based in Jerusalem.** God burns their city and kills them (Matt 22). In John's Gospel, "the Jews" oppose God's agent Jesus. (To be fair, Paul's vision is of "all Israel" included in God's mercy.)

- **God is constructed as having a mixed record on gender matters.** Generally, the Gospels foreground male disciples, though some women, like Mary, have prominent roles, and Romans 16 includes some women leaders. First and Second Timothy reinscribe patriarchal household structures in God's house/hold.

- With regard to social structures, **God is constructed as talking a big game but not delivering.** While Mary and then Jesus proclaim God's overturning of the unjust power structures, the world remains unchanged. Likewise, Jesus's disciples pray consistently for God to hallow God's name and establish God's reign, only for the status quo to remain in place. While James announces God's partiality to the poor, the rich continue unhindered and the poor remain poor.

- **God is constructed as uncaring, powerless, and indifferent to suffering.** In fact, God causes suffering. While God selectively protects Jesus, baby boys around Bethlehem die. While 1 John's small community is identified as the children of God, the rest of the world is consigned to the devil as the devil's children. While one man at the pool gets healed, many do not (John).

- **God is constructed as a paradox**, an opponent of imperial power thwarting Herod with his death (Matt), bringing down the mighty (Luke), destroying Rome's empire (Rev), and opposing "the world" (Jas) and the Roman-allied Jerusalem elite (Luke, Matt, Mark), yet also as an imitator in exercising violence, maintaining slaves, imposing God's rule over the world, and condemning opponents.

Conclusion?

These and other matters raise **Red flags** about constructions of God in the New Testament (or at least in the sample of the fifteen texts discussed above). There is no space here to address each of these issues, let alone "solve" them. But a first step is to notice that such troubling constructions exist in the New Testament texts and to be disturbed that these constructions exist in this religious tradition. A further step is to understand how and from where such constructions emerged in the tradition. Another step is to "proceed with caution" and enter into a process of discerning which parts of the tradition can be usefully carried forward and which parts should be revised or left behind.

Questions for Reflection/Discussion

1. Review the seven different ways of talking about God identified in the fifteen texts. Which one(s) do you find most helpful in thinking about God?

2. Does anything surprise you about the six areas of life in which God is at work?

3. Discuss the red-flag issues. Which ones do you particularly find disturbing and why?

4. How does what you have thought about in this book engage or challenge your thinking about God?

5. A recent book has suggested that Americans have four dominant understandings of God: authoritative (engaged with humans and judgmental), benevolent (loving and helpful), critical (catalogues sin but without punishment), distant (stands apart from the world). Which option do you align with most? How do you think such understandings of God impact how people live and act?[2]

Notes

1. Introduction

1. Karen Armstrong, *A History of God: The 4000-Year Quest of Judaism, Christianity, and Islam* (New York: Ballantine Books, 1993).

2. Nils Dahl, "The Neglected Factor in New Testament Theology," *Reflections* 75 (1975): 5–8. The essay was reprinted in Donald Juel, ed., *Jesus the Christ: The Historical Origins of Christological Doctrine* (Minneapolis: Fortress, 1991), 120–40.

3. Donald Guthrie, *New Testament Theology* (Downers Grove, IL: InterVarsity, 1981), 75–115.

4. Andrew Das and Frank Matera, eds., *The Forgotten God: Perspectives in Biblical Theology* (Louisville: Westminster John Knox, 2002); Jerome H. Neyrey, *Render to God: New Testament Understandings of the Divine* (Minneapolis: Fortress, 2004).

5. Larry Hurtado, *God in New Testament Theology* (Nashville: Abingdon, 2010). Hurtado (1–26) offers a good overview of previous scholarship on God in the NT and employs a "proto-trinitarian" framework.

6. On Jesus or Christology, see the forthcoming book in this series: David Bartlett, *Christology in the New Testament* (Nashville: Abingdon, 2017).

7. Phyllis Trible, *Texts of Terror: Literary-Feminist Readings of Biblical Narratives* (Philadelphia: Fortress, 1984).

8. Two recent discussions have attacked the existence of God and presentations of God in the Bible. Richard Dawkins, *The God Delusion* (Boston: Mariner/Bantam, 2006); and Christopher Hitchens, *God Is Not Great: How Religion Poisons Everything* (New York: Twelve, 2007).

3. God: Ultra Generous and Ultra Judgmental

1. For texts see Josephus, *Jewish War* 5.559; 6.96-111, 409-11; 7.323-36; *4 Ezra* 2–5; *2 Baruch* 1:1-5; 4:1; 6:9; 32:2-3.

4. The Good News and Empire of God

1. We can note *Psalms of Solomon* 17 where the anointed one is from the line of David and his task is to dismiss the Romans from Jerusalem "by the word of his mouth." In *1 Enoch* 37–71, the "anointed one" is a heavenly judge who is active with God in the final judgment especially against powerful oppressive rulers. In the Dead Sea Scrolls found at Qumran, there were several awaited anointed figures including a priestly and kingly figure. In *4 Ezra*, the "anointed one" rules the earth for four hundred years, then dies, then after seven days of silence God establishes a new heaven and earth.

2. Philostratus, *Life of Apollonius of Tyana*, 5.8.

3. Plutarch, *Life of Pompey*, 66.

4. Augustus, *Res Gestae*, 32.

7. Praying to What Sort of God?

1. Three NT references refer to God as Father with the Aramaic word "Abba" (Mark 14:36; Rom 8:15; Gal 4:6). It used to be thought that this word was uniquely used by Jesus for God, used by kids for their fathers, and meant "Daddy." None of these claims is true. The word did express closeness.

2. Gail O'Day, "John," in *Women's Bible Commentary: Expanded Edition*, ed. Carol Newsom and Sharon Ringe (Louisville: Westminster John Knox, 1998), 392–93.

3. Warren Carter, *The Roman Empire and the New Testament: An Essential Guide* (Nashville: Abingdon, 2006), 109–18.

4. Matthew's seventh petition, "but rescue us from the evil one," elaborates this third option. God would not bring people to "the time of trial" of despair and hopelessness if God acted to put the evil one (the devil or Satan) out of business.

5. NIV strangely translates the word as "boldness." This too is not an accurate translation. The CEB renders this as "brashness."

8. How to Dishonor God

1. For example, read 1 Maccabees 2:27-41, where Jewish fighters refuse to fight on the Sabbath as a day of rest. Many are slaughtered along with their wives, children,

and livestock. The survivors reconsider this observance of Sabbath and decide they will fight on the Sabbath if attacked.

2. Some translations, like the CEB, render this as "the Jewish leaders" to highlight this distinction.

3. See the moving accounts in Stephen V. Sprinkle, *Unfinished Lives: Reviving the Memories of LGBTQ Hate Crimes Victims* (Eugene, OR: Resource/Wipf and Stock, 2011).

9. Cornelius, Peter, and an (Im)partial God

1. Galatians 2:11-14 presents a very different picture of Peter/Cephas. There is not space here to discuss this issue. I will focus only on Acts 10–11.

2. For example, Peter heals a crippled beggar (Acts 3:1-10), the apostles heal many (Acts 5:12-16), a group is chosen to provide food for widows (Acts 6:1-6), Peter heals and raises a dead man (Acts 9:32-42), the church in Antioch provides relief for the church in Judea during famine (Acts 11:27-30), and Paul heals and casts out spirits (Acts 19:11-12).

10. God Does Not Play Well with Other Gods

1. But note verses like Pss 9:11; 68:16; 132:13-14 that declare God has chosen to reside in Zion/Jerusalem and its temple. Jeremiah 7 warns against misplaced trust in God's presence in the temple in Jerusalem.

2. The election of Israel is not a rejection of all other nations. Israel as a "light to the nations" is a means of reaching the nations (Isa 42:6).

11. God Doesn't Throw Thunderbolts

1. See the discussion of the same phrase in Mark 1:14 in chapter 4 above. The term could refer to political events as well as God acting to deliver people from Babylonian tyranny (Isa 40:9-10; 52:6-10).

12. God's Love Wins?

1. See chapter 4 on Mark 15 above.

13. The Household of God and Its Male Guardians

1. See the discussion at the close of chapter 12 above.

15. All You Need Is Love?

1. On God and prayer, see chapter 7 above on Luke 11.

16. God on the Throne

1. I elaborate this approach in Warren Carter, *What Does Revelation Reveal? Unlocking the Mystery* (Nashville: Abingdon, 2011).

17. Conclusion?

1. Brad J. Bushman et al., "When God Sanctions Killing: Effect of Scriptural Violence on Aggression," *Psychological Science* 18 (March 2007): 204–7, esp. 206–7.

2. Paul Froese and Chris Bader, *America's Four Gods: What We Say about God and What That Says About Us*, 2nd ed. (New York: Oxford University Press, 2015).